DIALYSIS INCREASES YOUR TEST SCORES

This Book Is Designed For:
Dialysis Technicians Nurses & Patients

WALKER GUERRIER

outskirtspress
DENVER, COLORADO

Dialysis Essential Increases Your Test Scores
This Book Is Designed For: Dialysis Technicians Nurses & Patients
All Rights Reserved.
Copyright © 2015 Walker Guerrier
v1.0 r1.0

Outskirts Press, Inc.
http://www.outskirtspress.com

ISBN: 978-1-4787-5016-1

Outskirts Press and the "OP" logo are trademarks belonging to Outskirts Press, Inc.

PRINTED IN THE UNITED STATES OF AMERICA

CONTENTS

DIALYSIS ESSENTIALS PART 1

What Every Dialysis Technician Should Know

When I was 22 years old, I worked in Manhattan as food purchasing manager for one of the best hospitals downtown. I had seven employees. When we were not too busy, we talked about our girls—some of us were not married— and we talked about food, movies, sports, and health. There particular employee whom we called The Big Man, who talked about everything and would eat all types of food. He was about 240 pounds and was 60 years old.

One Monday he came to work complaining of dizziness chest pain, and thought he was going to have a stroke or heart attack. I immediately told him he should leave right away to go see his doctor, but he refused. Three weeks later he went to his doctor and found out his blood pressure was high, and his kidneys were not functioning at all. He went on dialysis. What made him go see a doctor that day was he dropped down with a heart attack. I saved his life by cutting a water hose, inserting it down his mouth, and with my hand I pushed down on his chest to push air into his lungs. After three minutes he opened his eyes— he had nearly died.

That was my first encounter with a future dialysis patient, and I never realized that high blood pressure and complications from kidney failure caused him to have heart failure. We all thought that was the end for him. One of the employees I was fond of could not continue his duties due to this event.

We all went to see him at home and he told us his doctor informed him his condition was so serious that he might have just a few months to live, and more tests needed to be done to find out the cause of his condition. Later on, he found out he was also diabetic. I went home thinking about his condition and that he had only a few months or few weeks to be with his loved ones. I thought about how hard this must be for his family. His doctor informed him he should go on dialysis to ease his pain and suffering so that he could enjoy the remaining months and weeks he had left.

This doctor helped him by having him work with a team of dialysis techs who would dialyze him, a nurse, and a dietitian. These four professionals restored his health. Seven years later, his 45-year-old wife called me to say she was pregnant by him. When I asked to talk with him, his wife said he went to play basketball with his friends. Dialysis had put new life in his body.

When the industry I was in went down, I wanted to understand how a team of four professionals had saved my friend from dying. There I came to understand how vital dialysis is in promoting a dialysis patient's life. I learned that working with the best techs, nurses, doctors, and dietitians is vital. As a technician what is it that we do that is so important, that helps promote patient health.

Technicians must have extensive training, pass a state exam, be physically and mentally strong, and understand their role in helping keep the patient well. A technician is the ultimate guardian of a patient's well - being. He or she sees his patients three times a week and communicates with the patient; this is the person who really can inform a dialysis patient. To clean the blood, a dialysis technician must fully comprehend a patient's vascular access. It is vital to comprehend the meaning of strong blood flow, these are the reasons why. To remove **particles, chemical imbalances, and fluid** since the kidney can no longer perform these duties, an **access** becomes one of the most important element to obtain these elements from the blood stream. An access is made with a vein or artery, often in the hands or legs, or sometimes a catheter is needed. A technician must be vigilant because this is where all particles and fluid removal occurs. The technician must understand that an access is like the garage at your house. This is where particles exit the patient's body. Often the patient's blood flow will decrease, and from that moment on a vigilant technician will communicate this observation with the nurse on the floor. She must immediately inform the patient so that intervention can occur. Understand that this is normal—an access is not a kidney. Sometimes, particles may be collected in the access, and that is why a routine intervention is crucial. This is where the technician plays a key role in helping his or her patient. The vigilant tech will feel and listen to the sound of an access; an experienced technician will sense if the blood flow is diminishing and know intervention is needed. Based on my experience I would hear a certain sound, and when I felt the access there was a strong vibration. From that moment on you should start preparing the patient access with antiseptic and prepare to insert the needles. This technique is vital for a technician to master and understand. If you hear one sure, you should inform your charge nurse.

For hemodialysis treatment to occur, needles are inserted in the patient access, blood flows through a blood line and into an artificial kidney, which we also call a dialyzer. The artificial kidney cleans the blood and returns the clean blood to the patient. The dialyzer has a semipermeable membrane which permits particles and water through, but keeps blood cells in. A dialyzer is also known as an artificial kidney. Particles and water go through the membrane into an important fluid called dialysate and some substances pass from the dialysate and emerge in the patient's blood.

The most valuable employees on the dialysis floor, I compare to a super computer and an owl; they are always on the alert, using their experiences to perceive and intervene, and using their keen sense of perception to help their patient. These are the characteristics I would observe on these vigilant technicians. When the regular computer fails, the technician is the one who communicates with the patient, makes sure the patient is comfortable, records any statement made by the patient, and keeps track of the patient's well-being while the patient is on the unit. That is why a technician is a valuable asset. Not all technicians possess these qualities; some just don't care, and look at the profession as just a job. However, in general, most techs do care for the well-being of their patients. If you are reading this book, you are either a dialysis technician a nurse or a doctor who cares and wants to keep abreast of the current trends in this profession.

Did you know? Treatment of end-stage renal disease has become a large-scale undertaking. The size of the treated population and the associated costs are not well-qualified. During the year 2000, the estimated global maintenance dialysis population was just over 1.1 million patients. The size of this population is at just over 1.1 million patients. The size of this population has been expanding at a rate of 7% per year. We do not have enough dialysis units if the trend continues. This is a good profession to be in if you are someone who cares and you want to make a difference for someone who has (ESRD). <u>If the current trends in ESRD prevalence continue, as seems probable, ESRD population will exceed 2 million patients by year 2012.</u>

Did you know? There has been an aggressive effort to increase auto genous fistula prevalence, primarily from recommendations by NKF and the Fistula First Vascular Access Improvement initiative. Catheters remain an essential access modality for a large percentage of the hemodialysis population. Tunnelled dialysis catheters or chronic catheters are associated with a multitude of complications. As a technician who sees the patient three times a week, you should encourage your patient to obtain a fistula or a graft as soon as they can.

<u>Do you know what dialysis is?</u> Dialysis is a medical process that is used when a person's kidneys are damaged and can no longer filter toxins from the blood. There are two kinds of dialysis:

Hemodialysis is done at a dialysis center. A dialysis machine filters the blood and infuses it back into the body. It's a 3- or 4- hour process that must be done 2 or 3 times a week. People on dialysis usually have a port or shunt surgically implanted into their arm or chest for use with the dialysis machine.

Peritoneal dialysis can be done at home. It requires a strong level of commitment because it must be done every day.

Nephrons are very important in the kidneys. Usually if a large number of them are damaged, this could cause serious kidney problems or kidney failure, and the result could cause complications, which include nausea, vomiting, mental changes, sleep disturbance, itching, loss of appetite, skin disorders, dyspnea, anemia, salt retention, hypertention, nocturia, and proteinuria.

First, we need to understand the kidneys are well-designed. Whoever or whatever created these kidneys had put in some serious imagination for our well-being, and this is what the kidneys do to keep us healthy. They are working 24/7 days nonstop. When patients come for treatment, our objective as a team is to do our best to help our patient, and our main objectives are clearance and fluid removal. To control the electrolyte level we help our patient with the aid of our dialysis machine. We do our best to stabilize electrolytes in the blood stream.

Electrolytes: The kidneys play an important role in regulating electrolytes in the blood stream. This is where a dialysis doctor comes in, constantly analyzing the electrolyte level. Regular blood testing is vital, and our teams seem to be doing an excellent job in this area. Electrolytes are charged particles like potassium, calcium, sodium, magnesium, and chloride ions. They are in dialysate in similar to the level found in the patient's blood level. For example if the level of a certain ion is low, we monitor this finding closely and make sure our patient has the right amount of ion.

We also help the electrolyte level in in our patient's blood stream by changing the composition of the dialysate. Dialysate is a solution in which water is the solvent and glucose is the solute. At this point we create a solution, which is a combination of solvent and solute. The solvent is fluid, and the solute is a substance that can be dissolved in water. Bicarbonate is used, which contains all these electrolytes, and also the bicarbonate helps to correct metabolic acidosis in the patient's blood, which helps the patient to maintain a normal pH.

We can simply say the solvent is **water,** and **sugar candy** is the solute.

When I just started working in dialysis, a patient asked me what is inside the dialyzer I felt uncomfortable not being able to answer this question correctly, I said to this patient, "I will find out for you and let you know." A few minutes later, here came another technician who had been on the job longer. I felt relief that he would know the answer to this question, but he was not sure himself. A week later I founds a damaged dialyzer. I opened it, and inside was a semipermeable membrane. It was a flexible filter that looked like some type of a strainer, with microscopic holes that would allow a certain size of particle to pass through it, just like a strainer.

From that moment on whenever a patient would ask me, "What is that tube?" I would answer by saying, "In dialysis we use a dialyzer. Inside is a semipermeable membrane that has holes so small that only small molecules, such as urea and water, can pass through. The purpose of the small holes—or you may call them pores—is to prevent large molecules and blood cells from passing through the membrane."

I would also explain that inside the dialyzer there is a process where molecule or particles move spontaneously from a region In which they are plentiful into a region where they are less plentiful. In dialysis, the particles move across the artificial semi-permeable membrane, allowing the removal of toxins and fluid from the patient's blood as well as balancing electrolytes. Large blood components like red blood cells white blood cells, albumin, and platelets are too big to pass through the semipermeable membrane. In addition, during this process, urea is being diffused from blood.

Sometimes a patient would ask, "What can pass through the semipermeable membrane?" I would answer, "Small molecules such as urea and salt can easily pass through the membrane."

To simply explain this process think of the term diffusion. For example, let's take sweetened milk. If you take half a glass of water and add sweetened milk to the half glass of water, this is diffusion. This is the process inside the dialyzer—this is how we balance the electrolytes, by **diffusion.**

The scientific tern is the process by which atoms, molecules, or other particles move spontaneously from a region in which they are plentiful into a region in which they are less plentiful.

A very important process occurring inside the dialyzer is fluid is moving across the semipermeable membrane. I made the observation when I opened the dialyzer and soaked it in concentrated sugar water in a jar so. I concluded that this must be osmosis because when I removed the fiber of the dialyzer out of the jar, I noticed the jar of sweet water was empty; therefore I concluded that this must be the process of osmosis. As an inventor I admire the creator of the dialyzer. I admire his imagination. Most people take a dialyzer for granted, but this inventor had put some serious imagination to make this work for our patient. Based on these observations I must say with certainty that osmosis and diffusion occur at the same time inside the dialyzer.

Let me simplify: the movement of solvent through a semipermeable membrane from an area of lower particle concentrate toward an area of higher particle concentrate is osmosis. The difference in concentration is osmotic pressure gradient. The result is that the concentration of molecule becomes equal on both side of the membrane.

Did you know? Dialyzers vary in their ability to remove solutes from the blood, and there are three major components that influence the removal of solute. The dialyzers are different in their capability to remove precise amount of solute from a patient's blood stream during dialysis. This is known as **clearance.**

Based on my observation with the dialyzer, with certainty I can say most solutes are removed during dialysis by diffusion across a semipermeable membrane I strongly stand firm by this finding and this is not a hypothesis. This process of removing solutes is also known as conductive solute transfer—those of you in medical school will probably be more familiar with this term.

The second thing that occurs inside the dialyzer is that as fluid crosses a semipermeable membrane, some solutes are pulled along with it; however, what I observe is a process is the most effective way to remove larger solutes. This is called convection, convection solute transfer, or solute drag. To simplify this, we can say convection has the capability to remove large solutes.

The third process is all dialyzers have the ability to absorb materials to the dialyzer membrane. This is known as **adsorption.**

» **The efficiency of a dialyzer to remove fluid, solute, and waste from the patient is known as...?**

   A) efficient dialyzer
   B) good membrane
   C) absorption
   D) clearance

Fluid inside the dialyzer moves through a filter because of mechanical pressure. As we know, fluid must move anywhere there is a higher pressure to a lower pressure, so therefore the filter trap any matter that is too big to go through it. This process is known **as filtration**. When water is removed from the blood due to a pressure gradient across a membrane, this process is to remove excess water and waste product during dialysis, and this is called **ultrafiltration.**

We can conclude that when a doctor is considering what type of dialyzer to issue to a particular patient, the most important consideration would be the dialyzer size and membrane pore size, because the dialyzer's size determines the amount of surface area, measured in square meters available for blood to interface with the dialysate. The pore size will be the size and shape of the pores; these factors determine how much solute can pass through.

Starting treatment, the dialysis machine switch is on and treatment begins. The blood pump speeds the flow of blood from the patient, then the needle that the blood passes through is the primary restriction in the circuit because the blood pump is pulling. The pressure created is a **negative pressure—**a pressure which is less than zero.

I opened the dialyzer because I was curious; I wanted to know what was inside. As a child I would open any gift I was given Just to know what was inside. As I open it I noticed there were two compartments: the blood compartment and the dialysate compartment. The semipermeable membrane separates the two compartments and the membrane was enclosed in a plastic case that holds the dialyzer together and provides a way for blood and dialysate to travel in and out of the artificial kidney.

The doctor would choose a dialyzer for the patient according the patient's individual needs, and there are three main type of dialyzers which are conventional, high-efficiency, and high-flux. The difference between the three dialyzers are that with the conventional dialyzer, you most likely would find it with a patient who does home dialysis. The high-efficiency dialyzer must be used with an ultrafiltration control dialysis machine. Hollow fiber dialyzers are good for controlled and predictable diffusion.

One of the most important fluids you will find during dialysis is **dialysate.** The patient's blood is in one side of the semipermeable membrane, in the blood compartment, and the dialysate is on the other side. When I opened a dialyzer I poured a glass of Pepsi inside and a cup of Sprite. These two colorful drinks did not mix. There are many factors that make dialysate important; this fluid helps remove uremic such as urea, and creatinine, an excess electrolyte and dialysate solution contain the desired level of solutes the patient needs.

» **What affecst the dialyzer to remove and take out waste from the patient?**

    A) solution
    B) ultrafiltration
    C) surface area molecular weight
    D) blood and dialysate

There are many blood-borne pathogens. Pathogens that are a risk for dialysis patient and could as well be a risk in dialysis workforce include **HIV, hepatitis B, and hepatitis C.** There are blood-borne diseases and antibiotic-resistant bacteria.

Viral hepatitis or serum hepatitis is caused by the hepatitis virus. It mainly causes inflammation of the liver and can be transmitted through infected blood and body fluid, like kissing, and it can survive up to seven days or more on surfaces. Hepatitis can be acute or chronic. It is the leading cause of cirrhosis of the liver. In United States, about 1.5 million people are infected. A 1:10 solution of bleach and water can be used to kill the virus on most surfaces.

HIV attacks your body's immune system. The virus destroys CD4 cells. Which help your body fight diseases. HIV can severely damage your immune system and lead to AIDS. HIV treatment may also help to increase the number of CD4 cells in your blood, which help fight other infections. Isentress is a prescription HIV-1 medicine used with other HIV medicines to treat adults who have the disease. When I opened the dialyzer to examine it, I quickly realize this little tube would increase the life expectancy of anyone who has HIV, and most doctors may not realize this either. I have been observing people with HIV. Some are doing dialysis, and some are not. Based on my observation, the patients who are doing dialysis seem to be enjoying everyday life and look very healthy, and the ones not on dialysis are really sick. I truly believe this artificial kidney is very efficient in helping to removal uremia and other toxins from the blood. In my opinion, all patients who are HIV positive should do dialysis five times a week. Their survival rate would increase tremendously.

Did you know? HIV- infected patients with end-stage renal disease have a very high morbidity and mortality. In the last decade, survival of HIV-infected patients in the United States has remarkably improved. To determine whether similar improvement in survival has occurred in HIV-infected dialysis patients, their survival was evaluated by using United States Renal Data system database. Survival of HIV-infected dialysis patients in the United States was determined, and influence of year of initiation of dialysis, and demographic characteristics on the survival were analyzed by Kaplan-Meir method. The effects of above variables on survival were also examined in a Cox proportional hazards model. Identified were 6166 HIV-infected patients with ends-stage renal disease who received dialysis in the United States. Eighty-nine percent of the patients were black, 7.4 percent white, and 3 percent other. From 1990 to 2000, one-year survival of HIV-infected patients on dialysis improved from 56 to 74 percent and the annual death rates declined from 458 deaths to 240 deaths per 1000 patient per year. The hazard ratio declined significantly in patients who initiated dialysis in 1999-2000 compared with patients who initiated dialysis < 1990 (hazard ration, 0,49; 95 percent confidence interval, 0. 40 to 0.60). Survival of HIV-infected dialysis patients has remarkably improved in the United States. Once again, my observation were right.

The point I am making here is that HIV-infected individual would benefit, their life expectancy would increase if they were on dialysis. If you are HIV- infected and you happen to read this book, consult with your primary doctor before attempting this technique.

Dialysis patients would have enjoy a better quality of life if they were doing their treatment five days a week—do you know why? Well, the data we obtain today indicate that life expectancy has increased a lot. Patients who had weeks and months to live are living 15 to 25 years. Imagine if these patients were doing their dialysis treatment five days a week. Let me explain this to you so you can have a better understanding. Your kidneys are a pair of vital organs that perform many functions to keep the blood clean and chemically balanced. Understanding how the kidneys work is important.

What do the kidneys do? The kidney are bean-shaped organs, each about the size of a fist. They are located just below the rib cage, one on each side of the spine. The kidneys are sophisticated reprocessing machines. Every day your kidneys filter 120 to 150 quarts of blood to produce about 1 to quarts of waste products and extra fluid. The wastes and extra fluid become urine, which flows to the bladder through tube called ureters. The bladder stores urine until releases it through urination.

This why it is so important for a dialysis patients to do their treatment five days a week. Waste in the blood comes from the normal breakdown of active tissues, such as muscle, and from food. Waste is sent to the blood. If the kidneys did not remove them, these wastes would build up in the blood and damage the body. The actual removal of wastes occurs in tiny units inside the kidney called nephrons. Each kidney has about a million nephrons. A glomerulus is a tiny blood vessel or capillary that intertwines with a tiny urine collectible tube. The glomerulus acts as a filtering unit. This is great stuff—the designer of your kidney truly loves you. In addition to removing wastes, the kidneys release three important hormones:

— Erythropoietin, or EPO, which stimulates the bone marrow to make red blood cells.

— Renin, which regulates blood pressure

— Calcitriol, the active form of vitamin D, which helps maintain calcium for bones and for normal chemical balance in the body. Remember at when I just started doing dialysis patients, would ask me, "Why is my blood pressure so high, and why do my bones hurt?" Now whenever a patient asks, I explain that people who have healthy kidneys produce a hormone called **renin**, which regulates blood pressure. When patients ask you about their condition, try your best to answer and communicate with them so they feel reassured and safe, and explain to them that it is important to follow their doctor's direction and take blood pressure medication as indicated. After they finish their treatment ask them how they feel. Usually they will say that

they feel much better—that they feel like themselves again.

The point I am making is that quality of life would
have improve tremendously if these patients were
doing their treatment five days a week. Healthy kidneys work 24/7.

One day a patient told me, "Since I started dialysis
treatment I have a great appetite but I am not sure
what to eat or nor to eat." Try not to ignore your
patients. I would have a simple answer like **"Protein
is important to the body**." It helps the body repair
muscles and fight disease. Protein comes mostly
from meat but can also be found in eggs, milk, nuts,
beans, and other foods. I would explain that healthy
kidneys take wastes out of the blood but leave in
protein. Impaired kidneys may fail to separate the
protein from the wastes.

Some technicians tell their patients to limit the
amount of protein they eat so the kidneys have less
work to do. But a person cannot avoid protein en-
tirely. A dialysis patient can work with a dietitian to
create the right food plan and avoid food with high
cholesterol. I would tell them it is best to talk with
a dietitian, because a dietitian would probably have
more information regarding their diet. That way you
don't appear rude or ignoring them.

Some of my patients are anemic and some of them think is because food that rich in iron that is the cause. If you happen to have a patient who has a misunderstanding regarding anemia, this what I usually explain to them. I tell them anemia may start in the early stages of kidney disease, when you still have 20 to 40 percent of your normal kidney function. This partial loss of kidney function is often called chronic kidney disease (CKD). Anemia tends to worsen as kidney disease progresses. End-stage kidney disease, the point at which dialysis becomes necessary, does not occur until a person has only about 10 percent of kidney function remaining. Most patients with end-stage kidney disease have anemia.

When a person has lost at least half of normal kidney function and has a low hematocrit, the most likely cause of anemia is decreased EPO production. The estimate of kidney function, also called the glomerular filtration rate, is a based on a blood test that measures creatinine. I would explain that patients on dialysis who can't tolerate EPO shots may receive the hormone intravenously during treatment.

Some patients ask me, "Why should I take EPO (epogen) and iron—are not they the same thing?" Most patients with kidney disease need both EPO and iron supplements to raise their hematocrit to a good level. If a person's levels are too low, EPO will not help, and that person will continue to experience the effects of anemia. Some people are able to take iron pills, but iron pill do not work as well in people with kidney failure as iron given intravenously.

In addition to measuring hematocrit and hemoglobin, the CDC test will include two other measurements to show whether a person has enough iron.

The ferritin level indicates the amount of iron stored in the body. The **ferritin** score should be no less than 100 micrograms per liter (mcg/L) and no more than 800 mcg/L.

TSAT stands for transferrin saturation, a score that indicates how much iron is available to make red blood cells. The **TSAT** score should be between 20 to 50 percent.

The point you want to make to your patient is that a patient whose blood is low in red blood cells has anemia, and anemia is common in people with kidney disease. In addition, healthy kidneys produce a hormone called erythropoietin, or EPO, which stimulates the bone marrow to produce the proper number of red blood cells needed to carry oxygen to vital organs. Diseased kidneys don't make enough EPO.

I had a patient who asked me how dangerous high blood pressure is. I explained to that patient high blood pressure can lead to serious health problems. Most people don't even know if they have high blood pressure because there are usually no symptoms. High blood pressure increases the risk of heart failure, stroke, and kidney failure. In some cases, high blood pressure can be caused by kidney problems. The kidneys produce a hormone called renin that helps control blood pressure. If the kidney are not working as they should, they may release too much renin, which raises blood pressure.

Patients with high blood pressure need medicine to help lower blood pressure, which also helps to slow the progression of kidney disease. Two groups of medicines that lower blood pressure are angiotensin converting enzyme and angiotensin receptor blocker. Tell the patient to talk to their doctor, who will be able give more information regarding blood pressure and medication.

One particular patient in his late 70s looked at me and asked, "How old do you think I am?"

I said, "You must be in your late 60s."

He said, "No way, next year I will be 79 years old— and guess what? I have been smoking since I was a young man, and I still smoke up to now."

I said, "But you are on dialysis. You should not."

He replied, "So what? I have been smoking for a long time now. Does smoking cause high blood pressure, and is that why my pressure is always up?"

I said, "How long have you had high pressure?"

"Since I was in my late 60s. Does smoking cigarettes cause high blood pressure?"

"No," I replied, "but it can for a while raise blood pressure, and it does increase the risk of having other health problems. Smoking injures blood vessel walls and speeds up the process of hardening of arteries. Though it does not cause high blood pressure, smoking is bad for anyone, especially those with high blood pressure."

For many years the US Surgeon General has warned Americans about the ill effects from smoking. According to the Center for Disease Control and Prevention, smoking harms nearly every organ of the body. Therefore, smoking is not a good thing for anyone, especially if you are on dialysis.

Some diabetic patients are on dialysis. Diabetes

occurs because the body does not produce insulin or cannot utilize the insulin it produces. The hormone insulin controls the level of sugar in the patient's blood. It helps the sugar to migrate in your cells to help give you energy. If you do not have the right amount of insulin in your cells, you will not feel well and sugar will build up in your blood after a long period of time. A high sugar level in your blood can cause kidney disease.

There are two types of diabetes. If you have Type 1, the patient's body does not produce sufficient amount of insulin. The treatment for it is that a patient needs to obtain insulin on a daily basis. With Type 2 diabetes, the patient makes insulin, however, they cannot utilize it. This type of diabetes can be prevented. It is caused as a result of bad eating habits, and lack of body movement. Joining a gym is not a bad idea.

A patient once asked me, "How does diabetes damage the kidneys?" A simple answer to this question would be that high blood sugar can make the kidney to filter too much, and then the patient starts to leak a lot of protein in the urine. The presence of small amounts of protein in the urine is called micro albuminuria, and if the patient has large amounts of protein in the urine, it is called macro albuminuria. After a while the kidneys start to lose their filtering ability, and at this point waste products start to accumulate in the body.

If a person keeps diabetes and their blood pressure at the right level, the risk of kidney failure diminishes. The best way to lower blood sugar is to lose weight, eat less sugar, and avoid bad eating habits. While following good eating habits, some doctors recommend an ACE inhibitor for most patients with diabetes. I always suggest to the patient that they discuss this issue of diabetes with their doctor and dietitian.

Once a patient said to me, "I smoke and I am also diabetic."

"Well," I said to this patient, "according to what I have learned in school and information provided on television, researchers have long known that diabetes patients who smoke have higher blood sugar levels, making their disease much harder to control. Now a new study offers the most definitive answer. A professor of chemistry at California State Polytechnic University presented results from his study of blood samples. He found that nicotine, when added to human blood samples, raised levels of hemoglobin."

Then I told this patient I did not conduct this research myself. He can go to the library and read more on this subject.

A cure for diabetes patients— is it possible?

I had a patient complain that sometimes she couldn't feel her fingers and toes. I did not know the answer, but I remembered my grandmother, who used to complain of the same symptom. I told her it must be old age. The second time the same patient complained again, I called the charge nurse and informed her. She asked the patient a series of questions. One of the question was, "Are you diabetic?" The patient replied, "My doctor told me I have diabetic neuropathies." This was a term I recalled learning way back in college. Diabetic neuropathies are nerve disorders caused in diabetes patients. Diabetes disorders can over time develop nerve damage throughout the body. Some patients may have symptoms such as pain, numbness, tingling or numbness and loss of feeling in the feet, legs, hands, and arms. Damage to the nerves can take happen in every organ.

It is estimated that 60 percent of people with diabetes have no form of neuropathy. Patients with diabetes can develop nerve problems at any time; however, risk rises with age and with patient who had the disease for a long time. Diabetic neuropathy is more common in people who have problems controlling their blood sugar. No wonder my wife always prevented our children from eating too many sweets.

The point here is simple: prolonged exposure to high blood glucose causes nerve damage. The dialysis tech should comprehend the different types of diabetic neuropathy—they can affect different parts of the body in many ways.

Peripheral neuropathy, which is the most common, causes pain or loss of feeling in the toes, feet, legs, hands, and arms.

Autonomic neuropathy causes changes in digestion, and bladder function and sexual function. It can also affect the nerves in the heart, as well as nerves in the lungs and eyes. Autonomic neuropathy can also cause hypoglycemia, which is low blood sugar.

Proximal neuropathy causes pain in the thighs, hips, or buttocks and leads to weakness in the legs.

Focal neuropathy causes muscle weakness or pain in any part of the body. If you hear the term distal symmetric neuropathy or sensorimotor neuropathy, that is the same thing as peripheral neuropathy.

Not just renin affects the blood pressure. Autonomic neuropathy also affects the nerves that control the heart, regulate blood pressure, and control blood glucose levels.

With hypoglycemia, a patient has shakiness, sweating, and palpitations because blood sugar levels drop below 70 mg/dl. In patient with autonomic neuropathy, symptoms may not happen, making hypoglycemia hard to recognize.

Patients should always try to keep blood sugar close to a normal level. Maintaining safe blood glucose levels protects nerves throughout the body.

In my opinion, I think that patient should have a comprehensive foot exam each year to check for peripheral neuropathy. Patients who are diagnosed with peripheral neuropathy need frequent foot exams. Experts recommend a comprehensive foot exam assess the skin, muscles, bones, circulation, and sensations of the feet.

Patients with diabetes are more likely to have a foot or leg amputated than other people. Now we understand that many patients with diabetes most likely have the most common type, peripheral disease (PAD), which reduces nerve function in the feet, which reduces sensation. Together these problems make it easy to get ulcers and infections that may lead to amputation. The good news is that it is preventable with proper care and footwear.

Whenever a patient asks you what to do regarding foot ulcers, you should tell them to take good care of their feet and see their health care provider right away for more advice.

Smoking affects small blood vessels, and can cause Type 2 diabetes. Smokers are more likely to develop Type 2 diabetes than nonsmokers. Patient who are diabetic and who smoke are more likely than non-smokers to have trouble with insulin dosing and con-trolling their disease. The more cigarettes you smoke, the higher your risk for Type 2 diabetes. Regardless of what type of diabetes you have, smoking makes it harder to control your diabetes. Smoking makes managing blood glucose levels, blood pressure, and blood cholesterol more difficult, and it also greatly increases the risk of diabetes.

Smoking harms most parts of your body, the organs and systems that make it function. Tobacco smoke is highly toxic and contains 4000 chemicals, many of which are known to cause health problems including cancer. The chemicals are able to travel anywhere in the body that the blood flows, causing damage to many cells and organs of the body.

Smoking affects the brain, causing addiction, head-aches, and dependency. A stroke can happen when blood vessels in the blood become narrowed. Smoking causes irreversible damage to the eyes, known as macular degeneration, resulting in blindness.

The mouth is affected in many ways including cancer of the lips and mouth. Smoking and diabetes cause damage to blood vessels. People with diabetes who smoke are more likely to have heart problems than those who don't.

If blood vessels are damaged from either smoking, diabetes, or a combination of smoking and diabetes, the combination makes it harder for the body to heal. The combination of smoking and diabetes increases amputation and nerve problems. Don't ignore erectile dysfunction—it is now recognized as early warning sign of heart disease. Knowing this as a dialysis tech, you are in position to understand your patient better.

Patients who are on dialysis seems to have fewer complications from these symptoms. I think the reason why is that the **dialyzer removes most** of the toxin and balances the glucose in the blood, rendering the patient healthy.

Patients who stop smoking will reduce the risk of developing Type 2 diabetes,. There are many benefits to your health if you do not smoke, and you can help improve your diabetes management.

One day I came to say hello to one of my dialysis patients. I asked her for her husband, whom I had not seen for long time. She said, "My husband is very sick. He is hospitalize with a (UTI), which is urinary tract infection." According to an article I have read, 8 to 12 million Americans will develop a UTI in the next year. Most of these people deal with uncomfortable and dangerous effects including pain, burning in the bladder and abdomen when urinating, and chills and fever. In addition, many deal with these symptoms. Why is this important for a dialysis tech to learn? Many people ignore these symptoms for too long and suffer severe kidney damage that could be fatal.

Most of the time, a urinary tract infection is a result of bacteria, such as E coli, that get into the bladder or urinary tract. The bacteria immediately begin to multiply. Treatments for the infections are antibiotics that work to kill the bacteria. However, antibiotics also can hurt, because they kill good bacteria in the body.

My grandmother used to treat UTIs with herbal medicine. As you continue reading, you will learn about the herbal medicine, which you have seen in the supermarket, but you might have ignored it because you may not know what it is. This is why you should do your best to treat this infection as soon as you can. UTIs can cause the kidneys to fail. Recurring infections may cause scarring in the kidney, which can lead to high blood pressure. If you act in time, a simple remedy can cure your urinary tract infection in hours. Here is the herb you have ignored for years—you should have plenty of it at home. MY grandma loved parsley. She treated a lot of women with it and she also made a living with her herbal medicine. As you read this book, I am going to ask you for a favor—don't tell your friends about this secret; just tell them to purchase this book.

Parsley provides the urinary tract with apiol, which is a volatile oil that acts as a urinary tract antiseptic. To a cup of boiling water, add one teaspoon of parsley, fresh or dried, and allow the mixture to steep for 15 minutes. Strain out the parsley and have a nice drink. If you are allergic to parsley, don't use or drink parsley. Follow up with your doctor to make certain you treat yourself completely.

Now that you understand UTIs are nothing to mess around with, I encourage you to find treatment as soon as possible.

What you have learned here is that UTIs can damage your kidneys. Add parsley to your shopping list when you go to the store.

The invisible enemy. E.coli, a strain called 057:H7, can cause severe anemia, or it can cause kidney failure, which can be fatal. You can get E. coli by coming into contact with someone who has the infection, or from animals. This can happen when you drink water or eat food that has been contaminated.

If the infected food is not cooked to 160F (71C) the bacteria can survive and infect you. This is the most common way people get infected. The second way is from a dirty toilet. The bacteria can also spread from one person to another, usually when an infected person does nor wash his or her hands and you come in contact with them and forget to wash your hands.

What do you know about lupus? It is a chronic inflammatory disease. It causes the immune system to attack various systems of the body like the heart, skin, lungs, joints, nervous system, blood vessels, and kidneys. It is called systemic because it affects the whole body. A healthy immune system produces antibodies to fight against bacteria and other infections; lupus prevents antibodies from working, and the antibodies are no longer able to tell the difference between harmful bacteria and the body's own healthy cells and tissue. As a result the immune system kill its own healthy cells and its own body parts, causing inflammation and organ damage. The cause of lupus is unknown it has been linked to heredity and environment.

Women are more likely to have lupus, especially in their childbearing years.

Other factors that can cause kidney failure are traumatic accidents. Certain types of drugs may also cause the kidneys to fail.

Now that you understand the main causes of kidney failure, whenever a patient comes into your unit, you will have a better understanding of the factors that cause them to have kidney failure.

If you are truly serious about your profession and want to do well on your state exam, read on. I am going to ask you for another favor—please don't pass on this book. Simply ask your friends to purchase it, and tell them that this book contains valuable information inside.

Dialysis Actual

This part deals with what we do from 5 a.m. to 7 p.m. This is not a book that gives you hypothetical situations; this part is about real life. Imagine that your alarm rang at 3 a.m. You jump from your bed, turn on the hot water, rush out of the of the shower, and get ready for your patients. On your way driving, you are hoping your charge nurse put you to work with a vigilant tech. By now you should know the characteristics of a vigilant tech. Let me refresh your memory—a vigilant tech is a tech who works with you as team, for the benefit of everyone.

You arrive at the center, put on your uniform, and with a positive mental attitude you are ready to make your patients' lives better as you proceed with priming all your machines. Your patients walk in. You greet them, and ask how they are. The charge nurse on the floor assesses them and gives the okay to proceed. There is no time wasted because the kidneys inside their body are not filtering correctly, and these patients need your help. Three hours later a patient calls. You take a nice deep breath and look at them sincerely. They thank you, and you say, "You're welcome." A feeling of happiness rushes in your mind. If your whole day continues like this, you know that you have done a great job. The feeling of happiness remains with you for the entire week knowing that you did not have to send any of your patients to the hospital. In my opinion, I do not think hospital nurses understand the art of dialysis. Unfortunately sometimes for other medical reasons we have no choice. Whenever our patients return to us they seem happier to work with a well-trained staff.

For a future dialysis tech-if you are thrilled about saving people's lives and making a patient feel better, then this is for you. However, if you have no patience, if you are rude, vulgar, or love to fight, this is not the right place for you. If you are a nurse who panics easily and love sending your patient to the hospital, you need to find a job in a hospital—at the dialysis center, we do a much better job. Ask yourself why your patient can't wait to return to their dialysis center. I would never work in a hospital where they dialyze patients, and I do not understand this behavior.

Dialysis—Actual Life

From 5 a.m. to 7 a.m., the dialysis machine is live.

If you want to be a future dialysis tech, imagine as you approach your center opening the door. You greet your partner. If the charge nurse put you to work with a vigilant tech, you should sincerely tell him or her, "I am glad to have you as my partner today."

If you are not comfortable, you could always ask your charge nurse to assign you another partner, and if it is convenient your request could be granted.

The floor and your dialysis machine:
When you finish priming, you need to check all the parameters of your machine.

For example:

Arterial Pressure: 500 mHg 80 mmHg
You might see something like

180 mmHg 280

280 _____ 0

0

300 - 80

This is real life. At 3 a.m. I turned on the TV, listened to the weather, took a shower, and took my body temperature. It was 37C (98.6). using a thermometer in the mouth. The idea of body temperature can vary based on what I was doing. If I was outside and then walked inside my house to take my temperature it would change to 96F. It all depends on what activities I was doing. In fact, normal body temperature can vary based on may factors, which could be the age of a person, the time of day, and whether a person is physically active or homebound.

During the 19th century, body temperature was established by a German physician called Dr. Carl Wunderlich. He is credited with taking temperature readings for thousands of patients, and estimating that a body temperature of 37C was normal. I personally disagree with that finding. I strongly believe age and the activities a person engages in on a daily basis determines a person's normal temperature.

The question is what do we consider a normal body temperature?

Some studies disagree with Dr. Wunderlich's conclusion.

A researcher from Winthrop University in the US published a study in 2006 indicating that older people have lower temperatures, and also it can vary depending on which part of the body you use to take the temperature.

An active young person's body temperature is generally accepted to be at 37C (98.6).

The NHS indicates that a normal temperature is around 37C (98.6); however, it depends on many factors, including the person's age, what they were doing, the time of the day, and so on.

This is a most likely question on the state exam.

» **The body temperature taken orally should be ?**

  A) 97.8 F
  B) 94.6 F
  C) 96.1 F
  D) 98.6 F

As your patients walk in, the LPN or nurse will take the patient's temperature. As a dialysis tech, you may also take the patient's temperature.

5:00 a.m. live
Some of your patients, due to their medical condition, cannot stand up to obtain blood pressure. Others can. You take their blood pressure, because you already know that blood pressure can be a contributing factor in causing the kidneys to fail. The instrument we use to measure the pressure is a sphygmomanometer. This the instrument we use to measure the blood pressure is made with an inflatable cuff to restrict blood that is flowing in the patient's veins. There are some sphygmomanometers that are designed to be used manually; however, those require a stethoscope.

This instrument was invented by Siegfied Karl Ritter Von Bash in 1881, and Harvey Cushing made improvements to the device. It now widely use in the medical setting. The unit for measuring the blood pressure is millimeters of mercury.

For many in the medical field, the mercury sphygmomanometer is regarded to be the gold standard.

So therefore this is another likely question in your state exam:

» **The instrument use to measure blood pressure is a:**

A) tachometer
B) binoscope
C) barometer
D) sphygmomanometer

Cardiovascular

I had a patient who came in with a rapid pulse of 118 beat/min. The probable cause for such a rapid pulse would be hyperkalemia, which causes most patient to go to the emergency hemodialysis with 25 percent with ESRD on hemodialysi . Hyperkalemia should be considered in the differential for etiologies of wide complex tachycardia in dialysis patients. Early recognition and prompt treatment with calcium glucomate can completely reverse this life-threatening condition.

Many patients with tachycardia may have no symptoms or complications. Tachycardia definitely increases the risk of cardiovascular complications. Our heart rate is a controlled electrical impulse which travels across the heart. Whenever the heart muscle sends rapid electrical signals, tachy-cardia happens.

My grandmother who used to treat patients who had heart complication explained that eating 2-3 portions of vegetables a day was linked with a 20 percent lower risk of health complications. On the other, hand intake of fruit provided only a 10 per-cent lower risk of health complications.

On the supermarket shelf, you totally ignore us, however, we are more valuable than the rest. Guess what we are? _____ (Fresh fruits and vegetables.)

One day my grandmother asked me which is more healthy to eat—fruit or vegetables? Can you keep a secret? Please don't tell anyone. When you go to the supermarket you totally ignore this item, which is vegetables, offering more protective benefits than fruit. My grandmother claimed that vegetables are more beneficial than fruit, and she died at the age of 104 years old. You can guess what was on the table most of the time.

» **If a patient has a rapid pulse of 130 beats/min, it is more likely the patient has what ?**

A) hypotension
B) hyperkalemia
C) tachycardia
D) cardiovascular

5 a.m. live, preparing for your patients:

Most patients come in at 6 a.m. As they are coming in, you must be very eager to greet them and ask them "How are you?" You want to know about their day off dialysis. Usually patients answer, "Try having a day without your kidneys!" I understand their problems and am always excited to dialyze them. One of the things you would find yourself doing is make certain they have a decent respiration rate.

What do you know about respiration rate? It is calculated whenever a patient is at rest and is calculated by counting the number of breaths for one minute, by counting how many times the chest cavity rises. Moreover, there are many factors that could make the number of breaths increase.

Fever, illness, and some medical problems make it important for the dialysis tech to make certain a patient is breathing properly when obtaining a patient respiration.

The normal respiration rate for a healthy adult at rest would be 12-20 breaths per minutes.

If you notice one of your patients has respiration above 20, do not panic, but inform the charge nurse.

The charge nurse will evaluate the patient further, and most likely as you start dialysis for this particular patient the respiration would be back to normal range.

» **Normal range for resting respirations in an adult is:**

A)   4 to 8 breaths/ min
B)   55 to 65 breaths/ min
C)   21 to 60 breaths /min
D)   12 to 20 breaths/min

5 a.m. live. This is not book stuff, this is what you will actually be doing for your patients:
Preparing for your patients—at 6 a.m. you as tech and the nurse will assess the patient access to make certain the patient access is working properly. If there is any abnormal finding, the charge nurse will immediately inform the access intervention staff to arrange an appointment to make sure the access is okay.

Before inserting the needles, you need to know whether the patient has a graft or a fistula. It is important to know, because as you become an expert at inserting, you will realize that these two products are not the same

Let's explore a fistula. It is a connection of an artery and a vein. A fistula happens in the legs; however, this procedure can occur anywhere in the body. An arteriofistula is surgically connected for patient in late-stage kidney failure. Usually the doctor in our facility would do a routing check on the patient access to make sure everything is working well. If any staff on the floor suspects any abnormal findings, an appointment would be made because the treatment would be more effective. The reason for this type of intervention is that it maximizes the amount of blood cleansed during dialysis treatments. The vascular access should allow an effective large volume of blood flow in the patient access.

As a dialysis tech reading this book, you are doing the right thing. You must be familiar with dialysis language. It is important to remember that there are three types of vascular access for patient who are on dialysis: a fistula, a graft, and a venous catheter. You are going to hear these terms on your dialysis floor, so remember them and understand the difference among them.

What I have observed about a fistula it that it is far superior to any other vascular access. It is simple and easier for insertion; however, it requires advance preparation. A fistula requires a longer time to mature—sometimes more than a year. The advantage of a fistula is that it is stronger, more effective, and does not cause many complications.

» **Whenever an access procedure is performed for a patient who has good blood vessels, what type of access would the doctor recommend?**

A) forearm loop graft
B) arterio venous fistula
C) femoral catheter
D) cuffed tunneled catheter

5 a.m. live, real life on the dialysis unit:
You walk in and along with the nurse on the floor, you assess patient access. You and the nurse notice the patient has a graft.

You should know that a graft is a synthetic tube implanted in the arm. This artificial vein can be used as many times as needed for needle insertion and for accessing blood while doing dialysis. The advantage of a graft is that it can be used in a matter of weeks. The disadvantage of a graft is that it has a tendency to cause some complications, and a graft may need to be replaced sooner. If proper intervention occurs on a regular basis, a graft that is properly cared for will last more than 3 years.

The third access you would probably notice is a catheter:

For some patients who have an instant traumatic accident which leads to immediate kidney failure, a patient many not have much time to wait for a fistula or a graft, so a temporary venous catheter would be used as a temporary access.

What is a catheter? It is a tube placed into a vein in the leg, neck, or chest. It contains two chambers that permit a two-way flow of blood. Whenever a catheter is activated, needle insertion is omitted. This is the advantage of a catheter is quick immediate dialysis no waiting time.

The disadvantage of a catheter is that it is not the best for permanent access. They can clog and cause other complications. A catheter would work for many months or weeks, allowing permanent access to progress and develop.

They are some patients for whom a graft or fistula is impossible, so therefore, they require a long-term catheter. Special surgery would need to be performed and constant monitoring would need to be performed on a daily basis to make certain all is well.

What is a buttonhole? One day I asked a new tech on the floor, "Do you know what a button hole is?" He didn't know. By reading this book, you will distinguish yourself. If you absorb this material you will on your way to becoming a well- informed tech.

A buttonhole, is system where you would use a limited quantity of sites; however, you would insert the needles exactly in the same hole by the prior insertion.

The three major types of vascular access may develop complications. The usual complications are low blood flow and narrowing of the access. However, venous catheters cause the most problems, which would require catheter removal or replacement.

An AV graft may have low blood flow, which is a sign of the narrowing of the access. In this case the AV graft would need angioplasty, which is a system the doctor would use to widen the portion that is being narrowed. If this procedure is possible, the segment that is being narrowed would need to be replaced.

Complications are less likely with well-crated AV fistulas, which have fewer problems and are more reliable and better in quality. You can often rely on an AV fistula. In my opinion AV fistula is the best type of access.

Many patients will ask you, "What is the best way to care for my access?"

There is a lot a patient can do to care for the access. Any vigilant tech and nurse will check the access each time the patient comes in for treatment. I would tell the patient, "What you can do on your part is keep your access clean and use your access site only for dialysis. Don't wear clothes that fit tightly, try not to sleep on your access site, do not lift heavy objects, and each day check your access to make sure you hear a vibrating sound." You must remember these simple answers because your patients will ask you. If you are not sure, tell them you do not know. Never give information if you're not sure about it.

To conclude I would say, "We are your health care team in this dialysis center, if you would like to learn about how to care for your access, ask the charge nurse or your doctor they would be more likely to educate you better on this subject."

Now you understand the differences among the different types of access, as a tech you will start learning the technique of insertion. You must be alert and cautious there is a term we use called **needle infil-tration**. This usually occurs when the patient moves the access muscle where the needle is inserted, or it can happen usually with the venous needle—the blood traveling through can cause a positive pressure in the fistula. This increase in pressure can be a bit too strong for the vessel to withstand. In the scenario of leaking blood under the skin, this may produce hematoma. The most common reason is that the needle punctures the vessel and goes out the other side. Usually after a few days the hematoma site goes back to normal.

Although infiltration can happen, it is a rare event. At my center to prevent this we obtain a drawing from the vascular surgeon who also provides us with a drawing, and a description. This allows us to have a better understanding of the blood flow direction, and allows us to use the access better.

Placing the needles, **antegrade** and **retrograde**, we utilize this language to indicate the direction of the needles. The direction in which the blood is flowing is a predicament as to where the needles will inserted.

Unfortunately I have never observed or seen any patient in my unit with major complication with infiltration. Our team is well-trained to prevent it or intervene in time before it occurs. This is a technique that as a new tech you will master as you are progressing, depending on your level of alertness.

The reason is that the venous needle is always inserted in the venous return and the arterial could be inserted in the reverse direction (either direction). If the needle punctures the side of the graft or fistula you go out on the other side, or if you hear the patient state that the needle does not feel comfortable you need to assess the insertion site to make sure the needle has not moved.

In antegrade insertion, the needle is inserted toward the blood flow; and retrograde, the arterial needle is in the direction of the arterial anastomosis.

» **Which of the following will terms would best define infiltration?**

    A) delicate blood vessel
    B) high blood flow
    C) hematoma
    D) a needle tip that punctures a vessel and goes out the other side

The catheter access is dependable intravenous access that allows hemodynamic monitoring and blood sampling. It is of the most common sites for central venous access because of its accessibility and low complication rates, and it is chosen as a temporary hemodialysis site.

The reason why internal jugular venous access is pre-ferred is the low rate of catheter malposition and in cases that where you need reliable tip positioning for fast use—for instance, medication administration.

Catheter is the best access. Based on my observations, I would recommend it for long-term care.

» **Which of the following statements is true regarding catheters?**

    A) a long-term catheter is the best way to dialyze a patient
    B) a catheter is not easily accessible
    C) a catheter has a high risk of complications
    D) the internal jugular vein is the preferred insertion site for temporary and long-term catheters

I had a patient I was very fond of who was on dialysis due to high blood pressure and diabetes. She would come to the dialysis unit in a wheelchair, and her doctor had told her she would never walk again. The dialysis doctor put a team of professionals in place to help her, and after a year of dialysis she came in one morning without the wheelchair. This patient, whom everyone believed could not walk again, came in by herself. She gave all the credit to the dialysis team members.

She said that very same week she showed up to church on Sunday, and everyone was astonished. They hadn't seen her for a long time, and thought she was in bed dying because of her diabetes and the complications of high blood pressure. The patient said there was a great celebration, because she hadn't seen her friends in a long time. The following week, the church collected money to throw a party for her. "I couldn't have been happier," the patient said. "This was amazing for me." She has been doing dialysis for ten years now, and is very happy with the treatment provided by our team.

Sometimes patients ask me if it is possible for them to lose significant weight. I always tell them that if they follow their doctor's advice and work closely with their care team, many patients are able to return to their normal weight. Patients who could not see have regained partial vision. These are great things and rewarding to experience on a regular basis. The worst part is that when patients have dialysis on Monday, Wednesday, and Friday, you worry about their days without dialysis. Anything can happen during those days, and they may have trouble controlling blood pressure, etc. It's always a relief to see them again on Monday.

Another of our patients who was having breathing problems prior to dialysis is now very happy also. "I rarely have difficulty breathing," he said. He was another patient using the catheter.

Many patients notice tremendous improvement in their health. These were patients that were desperate, who thought they would never walk again. We turned their desperation into hope.

When the nurse and a technician are looking at the access before inserting the needles, they are always on the lookout for complications like stenosis, which can cause serious vascular access complications. The arteriovenous fistula is viewed as the vascular access of choice for hemodialysis due to the fact that it has fewer complications. However, stenosis is viewed as the major reason for dysfunction of arteriovenous fistula. In our dialysis center, we take the problem of access stenosis very seriously. We are all on the lookout for any changes in the thrill and bruit. Whenever we notice any changes, we quickly inform the charge nurse for early intervention, because stenosis complication is a predictor of graft or fistula thrombosisl and this could cause access failure. Angioplasty is a form of treatment to help resolve the problem of stenosis.

» **Stenosis can be a reason for access failure, and if not corrected in time it can lead to access failure and thrombosis and other complications. Which of the following term is a sign of stenosis?**

    A) stenosis
    B) mature fistula
    C) changes in the thrill an bruit
    D) low blood volume

In our facility, we practice good hand washing. It is not too difficult to do; simply understand the amount of time it takes to properly wash your hands. A good technique of hand-washing is the best way to eliminate your risk of acquiring disease, and to protect yourself from getting sick from germs. If you have a child or an elderly you are caring for, they are more vulnerable to infection due to the fact that their immunity is weak. When is the appropriate time to wash your hands? If you have a cold, after coughing sneezing, changing diapers, before and after treating a cut or a wound, and before preparing food.

I mentioned earlier, that the duration of time in washing your hands is important, and how you wash your hands is more important. Therefore, what is the right method for hand-washing?

Warm water is preferable because the heat in the warm water sterilizes your hands, and also warm water is a proven method for disinfectant; in addition, a good antibacterial soap makes washing your hands more effective. The best way is to first wet hands with warm water, second apply soap, and apply friction by using the palms of your hands and fingers together. Don't forget under your nails, which is a place that holds germs.

Continue this process for twenty seconds. The third step is paper towels or an air dryer.

I was watching a program on TV that they stated that if water is not available, alcohol-based hand sanitizers can reduce the number of germs on your hands; however, it does not remove certain types of bacteria.

» **Which is the best step to take in preventing yourself from getting the flu?**

    A) don't wash your hands
    B) don't use soap, just water
    C) only utilize alcohol-based sanitizer
    D) good hand-washing

Poor blood circulation: It is estimated that nearly 20 million or more people who live in Americas actively have diabetes. It is alarming to learn that many individuals have diabetes, according to the news. The reason for a diabetic patient to have blood circulation problems would be that increase of blood glucose can affect circulation. It is vital for patients to keep track of their blood sugar. Especially if you are on dialysis, blood flow is important to the dialysis tech, to help maintain good blood cleaning. Sometimes poor circulation can result from poor placement of the catheters and Fibrin sheet. To maintain an effective cleaning of the blood, a patient should have a minimum 400 blood flow, although a new access may not be able to maintain that much blood flow. With time and proper care of the access, a 400 blood flow is an achievable goal. For diabetic patients who have poor blood circulation, and those who lack of the necessary enzyme to help their blood from clotting, insulin seems to solve their clotting problem.

» **Lack of blood flow while doing dialysis in patient who has catheters could be caused by what?**

A) blood clot
B) a fibrin sheet around the catheter
C) poor placement of the catheter
D) bruit

Water and dialysate are important factors in doing dialysis. Microbial contamination is one of the factors the chief technician is always on alert for. Antimicrobial standards for water and dialysate were initiated by the Association for the Advancement of Medical Instrumentation (AAMI). They have set the standard for a limitation for bacteria in water at 200 colony forming units per (CUF/ML) and in dialysate at 200 CFU/ml.

What may occur in the future is that ultrapure dialysate will be considered a new quality standard for contemporary dialysis. A new survey has been performed on water and dialysate microbial quality in dialysis facilities in the United States and also in Europe. This has shown sown that compliance is not that bad. However, soon ultrapurity of water and diaslysate would be beneficial for ESRD patients and will be accepted as a new standard for more advanced biocompatible dialysis.

» **Based on AAMI standards, total microbial count of dialysate should not be more than:**

A) 100
B) 200
C) 100
D) 2000

» **Question**
Base on AAMI standards, the total microbial count of water used to prepare dialysate should not go over:

A) 100
B) 200
C) 300
D) 400

Product water must be monitored often to confirm that the water you utilize for the purpose of dialysis is in accord with AAMI standards, due to chemical contamination and bacteria. The sample water must be sent to a good lab that has the ability to check it using the exact system and the levels specified by the AAMI. Based on regulations, water must be tested each year. Each dialysis center must meet the AAMI standards. It is recommended that you test your product water quarterly or monthly. The sample for product water chemical analysis must be drawn from a sample port immediately after the RO or DI system.

» **Based on AAMI standards, bacteria testing for water and dialysate should be done:**

A) every year
B) monthly
C) weekly
D) every day

The complete water treatment system: Let me clearly articulate that this is a vital routine you will do as dialysis technician. You will check the water treatment system for chlorine and chloramines, which are put in municipal water system to remove bacteria. It is important to understand that for our purpose, we must ensure that they are removed from our water for the purpose of dialysis. I visited a dialysis center and I had the opportunity to talk with a few dialysis technicians; some were not sure how chlorine is removed from the RO system. This is a process to understand and it is important to understand how chlorine is removed.

Chlorine is removed from the incoming water by running it through tanks filled with granulated activated charcoal (GAC, or carbon). Like a sponge, it absorbs this chemical.

The carbon tanks are very important. They really function properly in a **series** of configurations. Allow me to articulate this process for you. Carbon tanks associate themselves with a pre-treatmen. As part of a water treatment system, water will travel first in one tank, which is the primary carbon tank—it is regarded as the **employee**—and a second tank, which is known as the **polisher**. It is important **to** understand that the quantity of carbon in your tanks should be adequate to permit the chlorine to be absorbed. Water should come in contact to the carbon for at least five minutes in each tank for a total of ten minutes for the worker and the polisher. This time is regarded as empty bed contact time, or EBCT.

To compute the volume of carbon needed, this is the formula V = (q x ebct) / 7.48

Let say you have a flow rate of 20 gallons per minutes (GPM)

If you want an empty bed of 7 minutes, your computation would appear like this:

V = (Q x EBCT) 7.48

V = (20 X 7) / 7.48

You need cubic foot carbon tank for each employee and polishing tank.

Therefore, we perform quality checks on the complete water system on a daily basis, and these checks are performed before the first patient of the day starts their dialysis.

The purpose of chlorine and chloramine testing is to ensure that chlorine and chloramine are removed form water entering the RO. The sample is taken from the first tank employee, and prior to the entrance the second tank polisher. If the first tank shows chlorine, then we check the secondary tank.

It is vital that the water system should be functioning for at least 15 to 20 minutes prior your first test. This will allow you to obtain an outstanding sample.

» **When do we perform quality checks on the complete water system?**

   A) after treatments are completed
   B) daily
   C) after turning on the water treatment
   D) before the first patient of the day starts their dialysis

Municipal and private well water: Perfect water is not possible because all natural water will have some type of microbial organisms, gases, and minerals. Some water bacteria are harmless and some are good for you. Lactobacillus Casei is known as the good bacteria. It enters your intestine live and neutralizes the bad bacteria. Let me share a secret with you—my grandmother used to treat people who had digestive problems, and she helped people build their immunity with this bacteria. Here in America we call it probiotics. According to my grandma, probiotics can restore the balance of the good bacteria.

Having a well-controlled level in your system aids to keep your digestive in good working order.

Some of the benefits of these good bacteria in water include helping with digestion and occasional diarrhea, help with gas and bloating, and supporting the immune system. Some of these herbal medicines are imported from the Island and, and you can find all these good herbal medicines in store here in this country.

Some of the bad bacteria in water, like Listeria, can contaminate people who drink bad unpurified water, and some pesticides and these bacteria can be found in water. Other bacteria is found in soil and water is Bacilli and Legionella, these bacteria can make people sick. If you are going to use tap water, boil it.

» **Municipal and private well water sometimes contain contaminants which are harmless in small quantity, which a person will drink. These contaminants are:**

A) soap
B) leaves that fall on water.
C) atmospheric gasses, and pesticide and minerals found in soil
D) chemicals

Tooth enamel protects our teeth. Putting fluoride in water at the right amount is very good at stopping the growth of cavities. Fluoride seems to have a great effect on tooth surfaces inside the mouth. Tooth enamel demineralizes If the water levels tend to have too much fluoride; therefore, defluoridation becomes necessary.It is important to maintain the amount of fluoride concentrate a 0.5 to 1.0 mg/L (milligrams per liter). However, it is imperative to understand that most water we purchase in bottle or gallon may not have fluoride, and adding a filter to tap water removes the majority of fluoride that comes in. The answer to the question "What is the main reason for adding fluoride?" is to protect your enamel and stop the formation of oral cavities. Most water treatment plants add fluoride at the municipal treatment plant.

» **This is added to public water and at municipal treatment plant:**

A) fume
B) fluoride
C) chemicals that prevent cavities
D) enamel

Let us have a profound understanding of the water we use for dialysis patients and why pretreatment is important. Allow me to articulate what we used to do in the past. Eighty years ago we simply used tap water to prepare dialysate. Understand that tap water is different in purity. During those days, patients who were dialyzed with tap water came in contact with aluminum, chlorine, iron, chemical compounds, and microorganisms. Today tap water is treated for hemodialysis machines. In this process we remove these chemicals and other contaminants. HCFA wants facilities doing hemodialysis to understand the guidelines, and tap water must be treated.

Water treatment systems must have a comprehensive maintenance program, which consists of checking conductivity, flow, water temperature, and chlorine level.

Nowadays, all hemodialysis clinics have a water purification system. Scientist notice an 80 percent increase in hematocrit level and fewer complications, and therefore, quality of life has increased a lot. What a difference! Technology is always on our side to help improve our quality of life.

In the past, the AAMI-stated maximum levels were voluntary, but now the health care financing administration (HCFA) wants facilities doing hemodialysis to comply with water purification.

» **Pretreatment water is important for dialysis equipment because:**

A) it improves clearance
B) microorganisms prevent ultrafiltration and expose to osmosis
C) reverse osmosis can be damaged by contaminants
D) patients are exposed to a large volume of water

Hardness of water—what is the cause? Some people think that hardness of water is caused by particle and sediment. But it is not really sediment, and particles usually stay at the bottom of the water. Furthermore, hard water is itself in its entirety is caused mostly by the quantity of dissolved calcium in the water and creates a hard scale when it is heated; however, some hardness is okay, to diminish corrosion.

The range of hardness water should be between 50 to 150 mg/l and this range will not affect water we use for drinking. Furthermore, sometimes hard water has a metallic taste due to the fact this type of water may contain iron and magnesium. The proper range for these metals is between 0.3mg/l 0.05 mg/L.

» **A large amount of calcium in water used for dialysis could result in what?**

A) hard metallic taste syndrome
B) formation of metallic particles
C) hard water syndrome
D) increase the strength of the hard water

A dialysis technician may work in a hemodialysis center where the dialyzers are reprocessed. Let us have a profound understanding regarding dialyzers that are reprocessed. You may hear the term "reuse" in some dialysis centers; whenever a dialyzer is reprocessed, there are numerous steps that are required for this procedure to occur. The steps are toclean the dialyzer, filling the dialyzer with a chemical call a sterilant called renalin cold sterilant. Then the dialyzer needs to be labeled. The last step is that the dialyzer needs to be rinsed prior to reused for treatment.

The reason why some facilities use reprocessed dialyzers is that the facility saves lot of money. Everything we use for dialysis has to be paid, for and cost of products is going up. As a result, some facilities turn to reuse dialyzers, which help them save lot of money. The cost of treatment is going up and the government pays the dialysis facility a an exact amount for each treatment. So therefore, the savings from reprocessed dialyzers are used to continue patient treatment and to purchase other important supplies that are for treatment.

The benefit of reprocessed dialyzers is that we help the environment. All dialyzers that are not reprocessed fill up our landfills. The disadvantage of having our landfills fill up with oil-based products and synthetic dialyzers is that they come from oil, a non-renewable resource, and they cause an increase in greenhouse gases, which can cause the earth's temperature to go up.

Whenever a dialyzer is reprocessed, AAMI standards want quality control activity before a reprocessed dialyzer is used. Two people should check the dialyzer—a patient and a nurse, to verify quality control information.

» **Who should check the a reprocessed dialyzer before use for dialysis?**

    A) a nurse and a technician
    B) charge nurse and chief technician
    C) a patient a trained personnel
    D) substance that kills microorganisms

Testing a reprocessed dialyzer: A dialyzer should have a very extensive testing to ensure it is ready. If there is any abnormal finding, the dialyzer will be will be rejected. One of the most important tests is a pressure test for membrane integrity. No membrane should leak. The reason for that is to avoid problems. The second test is the volume testing, to make certain the dialyzer retains its quality. This test is done to make certain that for the adequacy of dialysis. This allow us to know if the dialyzer retains 80 percent of its bundle volume. If it is less than 80 percent, the dialyzer will be subject to rejection. It must also have an aesthetic appearance.

Inside a dialyzer has two parts, which are the blood compartment and dialysate compartment. The function of the dialysate fluid does a superb job in helping to clean the blood. The entrance of the blood to the dialyzer is on the top; it travels and comes in contact with the membranes.

The function of the membranes contain pores that remove uremia from the blood—remember, I mention the blood is on top. Therefore, the dialysate also needs to enter the dialyzer at the bottom of the dialyzer. That is where dialysate fluid enters the dialyzer. Blood and dialysate move in deferent directions—as dialysate and uremia arrive at the top of the dialyzer, they are ejected to a drainer.

» **There are two main reasons for rejecting a reprocessed dialyzer:**

A) if the dialyzer is reprocessed and contain no description
B) less than 80 % of bundle and aesthetic appearance
C) not enough information on the dialyzer
D) the surface area and no description

5:00 a.m. live

You walk in and prepare to start priming. If this is your first time holding a dialyzer, you should read and understand the instructions in the dialyzer package. Your first temptation might be to think, "I read this book; let me go ahead and start priming." Wrong. You should read the instruction package insert, which will have a complete description, prior to priming.

The proper procedures for priming are: First put the dialyzer on the machine in the vertical position, arterial end down—or the arterial could be end up, depending on the type of blood line your dialysis unit is using. Attach the arterial and venous blood lines on the hemodialysis machine as directed in the machine and blood line manufacturer's instruction. It is useful to have a technician who has done it before to guide you. Second, be certain the covers on the patient ends of the blood tubing are secure, and put in the container for collecting saline, which is used for priming the dialyzer.

Third, remove the blood cover from the arterial end of the dialyzer and attach the dial end of the arterial blood tubing to the arterial end of the dialyzer. You would want to do the same procedure for the venous end of the dialyzer.

Fourth, you need a one-liter bag of saline solution and a clamped dialysis priming set. Fifth, put the dialysis priming set to the saline (T) connection locate below the blood pump segment on the arterial blood line. Open the clamp on the dialysis priming set and saline (T) to gravity prime the arterial blood line, and clamp the main line clamp on arterial line.

To prime the venous line, you want to turn the blood pump speed_____ ml/min as priming occurring there is a tap technique which helps to purge air out of the dialyzer.

When 500 ml of saline has been primed through the dialyzer and blood line, stop the pump and clamp the main line tubing clamp on the venous blood line. Blood lines connect the patient ends of the arterial and venous blood lines together to prepare for recirculation.

The last thing you would do are put the dialysate lines to the dialyzer. Invert the dialyzer, venous end down—the reason for this is that now you want to prime the dialyzer compartment. When the dialysate compartment is filled, return the dialyzer to the arterial-end-down position. If the blood line contains transducer protectors, connect transducer protectors and monitor lines to pressure ports.

From this moment, start the blood pump and set the pump to 400 ml/min. This will allow proper recirculation. Continue recirculation until patient until the patient ready to start treatment.

The main reasons for priming the line and dialyzer is to remove manufacture residue and to remove air inside the blood line.

» **What is the cause for dialyzers to be reprocessed?**

A) reprocessed dialyzers are safer
B) reprocessed dialyzers help keep cost of dialysis treatment down
C) reprocessed dialyzers increase circulation
D) it improves hematocrit

» **What are the main reasons for priming the blood line and the dialyzer?**

    A) to make sure the blood line is okay
    B) to rinse out residue
    C) to rinse out residue and remove air
    D) all of the above

Transmembrane pressure: Let's have a profound understanding in regard to the pressure inside the dialyzer. Here pressure needs a force or movement; therefore, removal of...? As I stated before, dialysis serves many different functions. The basic two functions are solute removal and fluid removal. We know solute removal occur mostly by diffusion. To simplify this, it is movement of solute from the blood compartment to dialysate compartment and across a semipermeable membrane.

Solute removal can also happen by convection; however, convection works well with high-flux dialysis and fluid removal, and takes place by a process we call ultrafiltration during the process of dialysis. If the transmembrane pressure is gradually changing, an alarm will ring to inform you. At this point you may suspect clotting. The first thing you should do inform the charge nurse. Most of the time, heparin will solve this problem by minimizing the clotting problem. If the patient cannot tolerate heparin, 15 cc of normal saline should be used to rinse the dialyzer.

> » **The transmembrane pressure is changing during the course of dialysis and you think the dialyzer i might be clotting:**

A) monitor the access every minute
B) look out for kinking
C) flush the dialyzer
D) all of the above

How to prevent infiltration? This information is valuable I would have travel to the end of the world to learn about it and educate myself on this subject. Notice that I use the word "how," because It took me a long period of time to master this technique. Although I have never infiltrated, knowing how to prevent infiltration is vital. First, promise me you are not telling this valuable technique to anyone—just tell them to buy this book.

For most new technicians, this is a great concern. Every tech that I talk to seem understand WHY, so let me profoundly discuss the why . Whenever a needle is not inserted properly, the needle enters the fistula, which is the first hole, then it makes a second hole and the needle is not inside the fistula. To simplify—more than one hole this known as infiltration.

The second thing you should understand is that the fistula or graft can blow if the access is new and the vessel wall is very delicate. The fistula can blow when the needle initially enters the fistula or graft .

Now, read on carefully—this is the part that took me a long time to master, which is HOW to prevent it. This is the part that will require your concentration. Look closely as you insert the needle to see if you have an immediate back flow. If there is no back flow at this point, ask the patient this question. Say, "I just inserted the needle for your arterial or it could be the venous— do you feel any sharp sensation?" If the answer is yes, you need to stop right there because you are inserting the needle improperly and you may ask the patient who has inserted their access before, and ask that person for help.

The third thing you should look for is a small swelling, or it could be a change in color at the entry site. As a tech, you should be alert and pay attention and communicate immediately with the patient, to would reduce the problem or prevent it. So therefore, monitor the patient access every time you have a chance and make certain the access site is in plain view. Tell the patient, "Do not move you arm or bend the access where the needle is in inserted, which could cause infiltration."

What is post dialysis-infiltration. This is where as a technician you need to be gentle. Post-dialysis needle removal is vital. This is how to do it to prevent post infiltration. Place the gauze dressing right on top of the needle. Remember this—do not apply pressure and remove the needle at the same angle you had inserted it. The reason for this technique is you will minimize the needle from dragging on the skin and avoid using the steep technique, which can cause the edge of the needle to puncture the fistula.

» **What would cause an increase in the venous pressure during the course of dialysis?**

    A) transmembrane pressure
    B) clotting in the arterial chamber
    C) a change in the arterial line
    D) venous needle infiltration

<u>Procedures and complications</u>

Renal failure :
Let have a profound understanding of the patient's dry weight.

You are going to hear this term often, so let us have a profound understanding regarding this term. Dry weight is a patient's muscle, mass weight which does not include too much fluid in the body.

There are several influencing factors and symptoms of water retention, including edema, swelling of the legs, shortness of breath (which could be water in the lungs), heart failure, and low levels of albumin which can cause water to leave the blood stream and go into the tissue, which causes edema.

For this reason, doctors educate the patients on this subject, including the avoidance of foods with a high sodium content. The dry weight is the weight the patient should be. For this to occur, a patient needs to follow the doctor's instructions, which include not drinking too much fluid and minimizing the portion of food. Dialysis patients may have too much intracellular fluid, which is fluid in the body cell. Extracellular fluid is fluid outside the cells in tissues, like the abdomen, chest, and legs. In most cases, dry weight is done by using different methods, which could be trial and error. This is where the doctor plays an important role in finding the dry weight, which in turn helps the dialysis team to do their job properly. This particular patient once stated to me, "I am close to my dry weight—do I need to more dialysis?" Being close to your dry weight has nothing to do to having more dialysis. You need more dialysis, if your urr or kt/v is poor. However, some patients may be able to decrease dialysis if urr maintain to 70% or more or if kt/v more than 1.4. Some patients may also reduce dialysis if renal function is improving.

» **Patient well-being is very important to all of us . Dialysis should control and limit complications of chronic kidney disease. What factor might indicate that a patient needs more dialysis?**

   A) if the urr or kt/v is 70
   B) if the urr or kt/v is 84
   C) if the urr or kt/v is more than 81
   D) low clearance

» **What factors would indicate the patient needs less dialysis?**

   A) good clearance, renal function is improving
   B) adequate clearance
   C) if the urr is 70 or more
   D) if the urr is okay

Let us give credit to the man who made all of this possible, through his research and his invention, a man by the name of Dr. Willem Kolff, who successfully created a decent dialyzer in 1943. The first miracle of the dialyzer occurred not too long ago, in 1945. A woman was dying of kidney failure and she was in coma. After 11 hours of dialysis she regained her mental alertness and returned to normalcy. This is a most likely question on the state test.

Principle of dialysis

During the first hour on the job as a new technician, you most likely will stare at the dialyzer, which is normal. Allow me to give you a comprehensive details about the dialyzer. As I mentioned before, there is a flow inside the dialyzer where we have the blood flowing and the dialysate. Patients receiving dialysis with a dialyzer can either have a countercurrent or a concurrent flow to clean the blood. The question is what is the difference? Countercurrent flow is more effective in cleaning the blood than concurrent flow when using a hemodialysis dialyzer. In countercurrent flow, the outlet concentration of the dialysate exceeds the outlet concentration of the blood. With concurrent the flow, that exit concentration is less than the outlet concentration.

In countercurrent, the flow maximizes the concentration gradient where blood and dialysate are flowing side by side. As a result, this system allows more urea—a lot of urea—to diffuse through the membrane, and that causes the blood to be cleaned more efficiently than concurrent flow. So therefore, we can conclude and understand that countercurrent flow allows for the most efficient uremic removal from the blood.

» **Countercurrent flow allows more for uremic removal from the blood because :**

A) blood is moving in a slow motion
B) blood and dialysate move in the same direction
C) dialysate travels through the membrane
D) dialysate and blood move in opposite directions

» **Which is more efficient, concurrent flow or countercurrent flow?**

A) countercurrent flow
B) conccurent flow
C) dialysate flow
D) all of the above

New technicians and nurses should comprehend dialysate delivery system— at least the basic factors.

I also believe that the dialysis team should understand how important these basic principles are, which we are going to explore as you read along. Be advised that as a new technician, you will meet nurses and technicians who are well-versed in this subject and they know their subject well, so therefore, the information here is important for you to read and retain. If you apply the subjects in this book, you will do well on your state test. I also suggest that you read this book as often as you can.

The delivery system, the standards for (HD) equipment in the US are put in place by the Association for the Advancement of Medical instrumentation (AAMI).

It is vital that the monitoring system be checked an calibrated on the schedule recommended by the manufacturer, and that conductivity and pH be verified by independent meters before each dialysis treatment and whenever the dialysis is changed, and that alarm system be tested.

For the purpose of having a profound understanding, I would split the HD process in half, which would allow us to have the basic understanding. The two entitied involved are the blood circuit and the dialysate circuit. By now you remember the blood and dialysate are separated by a semipermeable membrane, allowing water and solute to be transferred. During this process, the hemodialysis machine contain many detectors, controllers, monitors, and safety devices to make certain of a safe operation during HD. This permits the dialysis team to control the blood and dialysate circuits and allow us to monitor vital components such as ultrafiltration, adequacy, and dialysate composition. All these invention make our HD machine more advanced and allow us to better take care of our patients. Based on my observations, the hemodialysis team is the ultimate on the floor. For example, a vigilant technician from a far distance who knows his stuff, would walk up and say, "Sir, you are not feeling well, are you?" The patient would ask, "How did you know?" This skill comes with experience, and you must be alert and understand what to do. Despite all these advances, a well-trained tech is still the ultimate when it comes to monitoring the patients. However, these alarms that are installed in the machine can aid in signaling a problem, which allows us to act on time. One of the most vital advances we inventors create in our HD machine is program to automatically change to safe mode if there is any slight malfunction. For example, if the needle dislodged, the HD machine would alarm us, allowing us to clamp the arterial first, then the venous. In my opinion, this is a great advancement. Any malfunction within HD machine would alarm us so we can act in time to resolve the problem.

» **The dialysate delivery system has a monitoring system. It is important these system should be :**

A) alarm system should be tested, ph be verified by independent meters, and HD machine calibrated.
B) all HD machines are the same.
C) the HD machine is automatic and control, check, calibrate the machine itself
D) all of the above

The following are the HD machine performs before every patient is started on their dialysis:

Test:
   - Level detector
   - Blood leak
   - Arterial
   - Venous
   - TMP Transmembrane pressure
   - Optical detector
   - Conductivity
   - Negative pressure
   - Positive pressure

These are the terms you should know and comprehend.

These are some of the important alarms in the HD system:

- Hemodialysis (HD)
- Pressure Alarm   Diasafe test
- Dialysate Flow   Alarm
- Conductivity   Alarm
- UF   Alarm

One more external invention that has been introduced so that the dialysis team can safely dialyze their patients is a system we call CRIT LINE: What is it exactly? Well, this device is supposed to allow us to better comprehend the patient's dry weight. It gives us a new way of watching the patient's blood volume change in real time as the patient undergoes the HD treatment. As a result of the information we obtain, we are able to instantly and quickly intervene according to the quantity of fluid the patient's body can shift or refill into the blood from the tissues anytime. One more important benefit of the CRIT LINE it allows us to know with certainty the patient's plasma refilling rate (PRR) and how it functions effectively with the ultrafiltration rate (UFR} in regard to the dialysis machine. The third benefit is that it allow the patient to have a dialysis treatment with no unpleasant side effects.

» **One of the main benefit of the CRIT LINE is:**

A) it prevents the patient from feeling bad dur-
ing dialysis
B) it works well inside the transmembrane
C) it improves the function of ultrafiltration
D) all of the above

Whenever the CRIT LINE is initiated, there is a small computer with wire that is connected to the arterial probe which sends all the data to the computer:

At the start of treatment, you would have these abbreviations:

- HCT definition hematocrit
  normal range 30 to 33
- HGB definition hemoglobin
  normal range 11 to 12
- Time
- HCT level
- SAT definition transferring saturation/ this
  is in regard to iron level / this is to know
  the iron level.
- SAT normal range 20 to 50

» **What is the normal range for HCT for a patient on dialysis?**

A) 30 to 33
B) 45 to 60
C) 70 to 80
D) 70 to 85

» **The normal range for HGB for patient who are on dialysis is?**

A) 18 to 25
B) 11 to 12
C) 30 to 31
D) 40 to 36

» **This device is used to have an actual dry weight of the hemodialysis patient.**

A) countercurrent flow
B) ultra filtration rate
C) crit line
D) all of the above

Test alarm:

Level detector: A photoelectric detector, it can be done automatically using a peristaltic pump control by the blood level detector. If air is detected, the blood pump is switched off, and if there is a break in the venous line, the bubble trap will drain, and the fall of the venous pressure to atmospheric will sound an alarm and stop the pump.

Negative pressure could be caused by a closed loop, involving a pump, constricting valve, air trap, and the vent.

The pH: The recommended range is 6.8 to 7.6. Not all machines have a sensor to monitor pH.

Temperature: A heat sensor monitors dialysate temperature near the dialyzer and provides feedback. Temperature should be 35 degree to 42C.

Conductivity: The amount of electricity conducted within a dialysate and the amount of electrolytes concentration. It should be between 13.4 to 14.3.

Alarms will stop the dialysate flow if conductivity is out of range.

Blood leak detector: The purpose of this detector is that blood should not go across the blood and dialysate membrane. The blood leak detector is located downstream from the diaslyzer. If blood is detected, an alarm would sound which would deactivate the blood pump.

TMP: Ultrafiltration is controlled with the aid of transmembrane pressure (TMP)

TMP = PBO - PDO

Positive pressure: Inside the compartment of the dialyzer there is pressure, and this is due to the blood pumped inside the narrow fibers.

Arterial line: This is the blood to you will find in the arteries. It is derive from the left chamber of the heart and lungs, and it is light red in color. This where blood is being pulled from the body by the blood pump.

Venous line: The venous blood is dark in color. Venous blood carries a lot of carbon dioxide and has a lack of oxygen. In dialysis this is where the clean blood is returned to the patient's body.

In dialysis the difference is that arterial blood travels with strong pressure, and venous blood travel with weak pressure.

To be continued...

Optical detector: This is a detector that is used to detect foam. In some machines, ultrasonic sensors are used that are placed either on the bubble trap or on the line below it.

» **The dialysate conductivity measures what?**

   A) the temperature
   B) the transmembrane pressure
   C) total electrical charge of a solution
   D) total level of calcium in the bone

Clearance: Let us have a profound understanding of the factors that affect it. The patient must comply with the doctor's recommendations. Many doctors often stress the importance of taking their medications, encourage the patient have four hours of treatment instead of 3.5 hours, prescribe an efficient size of the dialyzer, and increase the blood flow rate. Many patient have a preconception of their treatment—some patients think that the dialysis machine is what cleans the blood. I inform them about the filter, and that the dialyzer is basically the one doing the work of cleaning the blood; however, the machine contains the components, such as the pump, alarm, and many detectors that aid in the dialyzer so that they can obtain an efficient treatment. Some patient are astonish to comprehend that. Some patients may ask you what is inside the dialyzer. Indside the dialyzer contains thin fibrous materials which form a semipermeable membrane. It is encased in a sealed plastic cylinder and it is a foot long, three inches in diameter, and it has an opening at the top and an opening at the bottom.

During treatment, blood and dialysate flow inside the dialyzer.

» **What factors in the dialysis treatment affect clearance?**

A) patient well-being
B) The dialyzer semipermeable membrane
C) the size of the dialyzer, time of treatment, blood flow rate, and dialysate
D) all of the above

» **What is the recommended range for pH ?**

A) pH 6.1 to 7.1
B) pH 6.8 to 7.6
C) pH 6 to 7.8
D) pH 6 to 8.7

» **The dialysate temperature should be how many degrees?**

A) 35 degrees to 42 degrees
B) 37 degrees to 40 degrees
C) 36 degrees to 41 degrees
D) 37 degrees to 36 degrees

» **The normal range for conductivity should be ?**

A) 13.4 to 14.3
B) 13 to 14.5
C) 13.3 to 14.6
D) 13.0 to 13.7

» **We rinse the blood line and dialyzer with what?**

A) normal saline of 0.9 solution
B) normal saline of 0.09 solution
C) normal saline of 0.9.0 solution
D) normal saline of 1.09 solution

» **Hematocrit normal range for dialysis patients should be what?**

A) HTC range should be 30 to 33
B) HTC range should be 40 to 37
C) HTC range should be 41 to 31
D) HTC range should be 45 to 31

» **What is the normal range for hemoglobin for patients in dialysis?**

A) hemoglobin normal range 11 to 12
B) hemoglobin normal range 13 to 14
C) hemoglobin normal range 14 to 12
D) hemoglobin normal range 15 to 24

» **The normal range for SAT for patient in dialysis should be what?**

A) 20 to 50
B) 30 to 40
C) 40 to 46
D) 36 to 30

The purpose of the extra corporeal circuit is to transport blood from the patient's access to the dialyzer and back to the access. The arterial pre-pump is negative pressure, and due to the fact that the arterial is under negative pressure, the extra corporeal circuit needs to be primed with sodium chloride solution to rinse the circuit and remove air, because the arterial tends to clot. Therefore, the negative pressure starts right before the blood pump. The most likely question on the state test would be:

» **Where in the extra corporeal circuit is the blood tend to be under negative pressure ?**

A) the post pump venous chamber
B) before the blood arrives at the dialyzer
C) the arterial line section before the blood pump
D) the arterial line after the blood pump

To clarify positive pressure, let us think in terms of how extra fluid from the blood is removed by the process of ultrafiltration. Pressure is highest in the blood compartment of the dialyzer at this point. Positive pressure exists whenever the blood is pumped in the narrow fibers. During dialysis, ultra-filtration occurs when water is removed from blood, because there is a pressure gradient between blood and dialysate. The pressure across the membrane created by the pressures in the two compartments is known as the transmembrane pressure. To sim-plify this, a positive pressure occurred post-pump, which is pressure between blood pump and dialyzer to detect clotting in the dialyzer. The HD machine has audible and visual alarms that will activate if positive pressure continues to increase. The blood pump would stop if the tech is not able to attain the HD machine. Another positive pressure is venous— if the venous pressure is positive, this pressure mea-sures the resistance of blood retuning to the patient, and an audible and visual alarm will activate if limits go up too high—or in most cases, the blood pump would stop. So therefore, the question is:

» **While doing dialysis, ultrafiltration occurs when?**

- A) the arterial line section
- B) high concentration of dilaysate
- C) extra fluid is removed from blood because as a result of a pressure gradient between blood and dialytsate.
- D) all of the above

» **When would a negative pressure be created?**

A) when there is a pressure
B) when blood is returned to the venous blood line
C) when fluid is pulled through a restriction
D) all of the above

» **When is positive pressure created?**

A) when blood flows inside the dialyzer
B) when blood flows in the blood line
C) when blood enters the venous needles
D) all of the above

» **What is the reason heparin is prescribed for most dialysis treatment?**

A) heparin minimizes clotting in the circuit
B) heparin prevents clotting in the circuit.
C) heparin prevents the venous chamber from clotting
D) heparin always prevents clotting

Let us have a profound understanding of concentration gradients— what are they? As our patients are connected to the dialysis machine, the concentration gradient plays a major role in restoring our patient's health. For instance, by now you should understand that the artificial kidney, which is the dialyzer, acts like a kidney to remove most urea and ensure the right balance of ion and electrolyte of the blood. The way all this works is that the uremic blood is taken from a blood vessel in the access with the aid of the heparin to minimize clotting, and returned into the machine. As I previously indicated, inside the dialyzer there is a semipermeable membrane where the blood flows in the opposite direction to the dialysis fluid. There the exchange takes place between the two, where a concentration gradient resides. Let us discuss the concentration gradients. The dialysis fluid contains a glucose concentration the same as the level in the blood. If the patient needs it, iron would be administered, magnesium, and so on. The way this works is that if the patient's blood is too low in glucose, glucose will diffuse from the dialysis fluid into the blood, restoring the right level in the patient's blood. For instance, if the patient's blood is too high in iron, the excess iron will diffuse from the blood to the dialysis fluid. Therefore, the logical question you would most likely find on the state test would be:

What will increase the amount of solutes that will diffuse across the semipermeable membrane?

    A) high concentration of heparin and glucose
    B) high concentration of iron
    C) high concentration of solute
    D) high concentration gradients

» **The movement of particles from higher concentration to an area of lower concentration is known as?**

A) osmosis
B) high concentration gradients
C) movement of transmembrane pressure
D) diffusion

» **The semipermeable membrane is a porous wall that lets:**

A) large particles to cross the membrane
B) allows uremia remain in the blood
C) allows certain sized particles to cross
D) all of the above

» **Countercurrent is effective due to the fact it removes large amount of uremia from the patient blood because:**

A) of TMP
B) of pressure inside the dialyzer
C) it allows dialysate to move in the same direction
D) blood and dialysate move in opposite direction

New technicians and **nurses,** how would you know if your patient would need more dialysis? There are many factors that would indicate that your patient needs more dialysis. First look at your patient's legs and ankles. If you notice that they are swollen, if the patient's hands are itching a lot, if there is vomiting or anorexia, if the patient complains of tiredness and being oveweight, these symptoms are dangerous and any dialysis patients who have the following symptoms would most likely need more dialysis.

» **Symptoms that a patient may need extra dialysis would be ?**

    A) chills, strong appetite, thirst
    B) swelling, anorexia, vomiting
    C) craving for sweet or salty food
    D) all of the above

New technicians and nurses will often hear their patients complaining that their bones are feeling weak. Let us have a profound understanding of the cause. Remember that in anatomy we learned the term "osteodystrophy"—or in dialysis we use the term renal osteodystrophy. The comom term on the dialysis unit is Renal osteodystrophy. Don't confuse yourself—all these terms indicate that the patients have bone disease due to renal failure. In my dialysis unit every month our doctor orders blood work, which in my opinion is vital. Let us look at why this so important. Patients who wait too long to take care of themselves can have their limbs, fingers, feet and so on fall off due to lack of calcium. Every month patients who are on dialysis must meet with their doctors or dietitian to review lab work from their monthly blood test, and based on my observation, our dialysis unit is doing an outstanding job in this regard. The lab result that are discussed are calcium, parathyroid hormone (PTH), and phosphorus. The reason why this lab work is important for us is that the health care team can control any imbalance in bone health, and for us to be able to give our patients mineral and bone problem management. By now you understand the importance of the kidneys. Now you comprehend that the healthy kidneys clean the blood of uremia and produce calcitrol, which helps keep bones strong. You also need to understand that the health of the kidneys also is a producer of certain hormones that help keep minerals in the body in proper balance and help keep bone healthy. We also learned that our bones help us to have good structure and mobility; they protect our structure. The skull in your head protects your brain and major organs, and so on.

What is most important is the fact that the bones in our body store minerals, which are calcium and phosphorus. These minerals keep our bone in proper structure. The reason for me to discuss this in great detail is because one day one of your patients will ask questions regarding their bone problems.

There are two types of bone of bone cells, and this is how bones are created: osteoblasts and osteoclasts.

Osteoblasts are cells that build bone, and osteoclasts are cells that consume bone. These two types of cells are in proper balance in healthy people to keep your body strong. These cells of bones are being built all the times. In patients with kidney disease, these two types of cells are not in balance and therefore, the patients have bone problems, which we call renal osteodystrophy. Let us look at why these cells get out of balance. Calcium and parathyroid hormone PTH) are out of balance, rendering these cells not to function properly, and this leads to osteodystrophy, when bone becomes brittle and can break easily.

» **What is the main reason kidney failure patients often have bone disease?**

    A) lack of magnesium
    B) lack of potassium and phosphorus
    C) lack of calcitrol
    D) all of the above

New technicians must understand the simple way to have a profound understanding of dry weight and the removal goal. Below is a basic comprehensive pre-assessment table. First we will start with DRY weight.

Pre-assessment:

- DW 87
- Pre weight 89.4 is the weight the patient comes in the unit.
- Expected removal 2.4
- Pre post prime 0.3
- Total UF goal 2.7

Post assestment

- Actual weight 87

Recall that I mentioned that the kidney is a producer of hormones. Let us have a comprehensive understanding of the other hormone the kidney produce that help keep us strong and healthy. Did you know that your kidneys prevent you from being anemic? Let us first understand what anemia is, and its complications. A reduction in red blood cells or being low in red blood cells is considered anemia. Red blood cells are vital for our well-being because red blood cells carry oxygen to major tissues and organs and into the body. As a result we are able to utilize the energy from the food we eat. Let us look at the complications of anemia. Since red blood cells carry oxygen to the brain, heart, and muscle tissue, as a result of anemia, a person with this condition may feel tired all the time. Patient with kidney disease usually are anemic do to the fact that the kidneys produce a hormone called erythropoietin (EPO). This hormone causes the bone marrow to make the right balance of red blood cells. Patients with kidney disease are not able to produce this hormone; therefore, they suffer from low red blood cells. This is the reason why monthly blood count is vital for us to provide anemia management. Complete blood count (CBC) is a laboratory test we take a sample of blood so that we can determine a patient's hematocrit level, which also indicates the amount of red blood cell a person has. The normal range should be above 40 percent and the low range of hematocrit 37 percent or less. Other tests are perform to check for iron deficiency. The treatment for anemia is done with a medicine called EPO. Some patients may not be able to tolerate injection of EPO. This medicine may be given intravenously while the patient is doing dialysis treatment. The US Food and Drug Administration (FDA) recommends any patient taking EPO therapy must achieve a target hemoglobin around 10 and 12 grams per deciliter (g/dl). Most likely the question on the state test would be:

» **The main cause of anemia of patient with kidney disease would be?**

A) lack of oxygen in the muscles tissues
B) lack of white blood cells
C) lack of platelets in the blood
D) lack of erythropoietin

The administrator gave us a lecture on buttonhole. I think as a new technician you should be aware of this new technique. Patients can self-cannulate by inserting their own needles. As a result this technique creates a tunnel From this moment on a patient does not need to use a sharp needle; instead a blunt needle could be used, which is safer. With a buttonhole there are fewer complications, such as less bruises and lower aneurysm and faster insertion. However, if a buttonhole patient comes into the unit we must make certain proper needles are being used and proper procedure is followed, for the well-being of the patient. The administrator informed us that we must establish some type of communication, especially if the patient is a transfer from another dialysis center. Proper communication with the patient is vital because the patient understands his/or her access better than you. This is the moment to find out how well-inform the patient is in regard to the access they have. You want to ask the patient, "Have you had any problems or complications, or is there anything I should know about your access?" That way the patient will feel that you don't just want to insert the needles and walk away. The patient will undertand that you are curious and academically want to learn and that show that you are a caring tech. A word of advice—a buttonhole is very delicate and efficient. The technician must apply all their skill when inserting a buttonhole needle. The most logical question on the state test would be:

» **What are the main advantages of buttonhole needles?**

   A) it is a sharper needle
   B) it is faster to insert, less bruises, low aneurysm rate
   C) must use caution
   D) all of the above

Let us have an understanding as to why the patient who has kidney disease often complains of itching.

One of my patients asked me why his skin was itchy. As a new tech, you will encounter patients with this condition. Remember basic health class and biology—people who do not shower often will develop itch of the body. It is vital to practice good hygiene.

However, for dialysis patients, this condition is a result of having a high amount of phosphorus in their body. Dialysis is supposed to remove phosphorus; however, the artificial kidney, which is the dialyzer, has not been able to remove enough of this substance in the patient's body.

Causes of itching for dialysis patient include the amount of food they are eating which contains large amount of phosphorus—this condition causes hyperphosphatemia. If the patient asks how their itching can be stopped, refer the patient to discuss this problem with the dietitian, who will be better-informed about what to do to help ease the itching. Most likely a diet that contain small amount of phosphorus would be prescribed. Most dialysis patientd are taking phosphorus binders with their meals; based on my observation, the patients who take their phosphorus binders do not complain of itching. The normal range for phosphorus level for dialysis patient should be 5.5. The patients who are able to maintain that range are the ones not complaining of constant itching.

Some people stated dialysis patient should not eat food that contains phosphorus. I disagree. Whether a patient is on dialysis or not, a person needs to have phosphorus in their body. Here is why. First of all, phosphorus is important for maintaining cell normalcy and aids in regulating and controlling calcium. In addition to that, lack of phosphorus may cause abnormal bone formation, weakness in immunity, lack of appetite, and muscle pain. If you need to decrease the amount of foods that contain phosphorus, remember the following. Some patients might ask you which foods contain phosphorus? The list includes peanuts, popcorn, ham,fortified cereal,wheat germ, cocoa powder, mushrooms,cheese, mustard, soybeans. Now that we have some understanding as to why and what we can do to maintain a proper level of phosphorus,the dialysis patient needs to take their phosphate binder to help minimize their itching. The most likely logical question on the state test would be:

» **What is the main cause of itching for kidney disease patients?**

    A) hyperkalcemia and phosphate binder
    B) lack of calcium and normalcy of cells
    C) hyperphosphatemia
    D) calcium deficiency

» **The normal range for phosphorus level should be?**

    A) 55
    B) 5.55
    C) 5.5
    D) 0.55

The kidney endocrine function:
Renin is an enzyme that is activated if blood pressure is low, which we refer to as hypotension.

Erythropoietin is a hormone that helps in the production of red blood cells.

Calcitrol is important. It helps raise plasma calcium levels. In addition, it is responsible for4 the activation of Vitamin D, which is controlled by the hormone PTH.

Let us simplify the endocrine function of the kidneys. The kidneys produce many hormones and enzymes. We also understand that erythropoietin is released if there are low levels of oxygen in the tissues. Renin is activated if hypotention is detected, and calcitrol is activated if the calcium level is too low. The most likely logical question on the state test would be:

» **The endocrine functions of the kidney would include which of the following?**

    A) control the level of potassium
    B) making cell tissue metabolism
    C) making growth hormone and mitosis
    D) making erythropoietin and calcitrol

The leading cause of end-stage renal disease for adults would be?

   A) hypertension
   B) hypotension
   C) diabetes
   D) all of the above

The real kidneys in the human body consist of this miracle worker known as the glomerulus, which provides the primary action in filtering the blood. All around the perimeter of the glomerulus you will find Bowman's capsule. Blood plasma is filtered through the capillaries of the glomerulus into the Bowman's capsule. The glomerulus receivse its blood supply from an afferent arteriole of the renal circulation. The resistance of arteriole causes pressure, which creates ultrafiltration, where fluids and solutes are moved out by force.

The glomerulus and Bowman's capsule around it form a renal corpuscle, which constitutes the basic filtration unit of the kidney. The speed at which blood is filtered through all the glomeruli is known as the glomerular filtration rate.

The tubule is part of the kidney that contains tubular fluid. The filtrate is fluid converted into urine, which exit the renal tubules via collecting ducts, which connect to a nephron to the ureter, where urine is excreted.

What is a nephron? The kidney contain more than a million nephrons that help in cleaning the blood. The nephron is the main component of the kidney, and does the majority of the work. It is made up of the glomerulus and a tubule. The function of the nephrons remove fluid and harmful substances from the blood and return electrolyte substances like calcium, potassium, and phosphorus. When the nephrons are damaged due to hypertension or diabetes, this leads to kidney disease. The result of this also damages the glomeruli. The end result of this is malfunction of the kidney. So therefore, the most logical question on the state test would be:

» **The nephron is composed of what?**

   A) red blood cells and muscles
   B) arteries and veins
   C) glomerulus and a tubule
   D) all of the above

» **The main component of the kidney that does the majority of the work is?**

A) glomeruli
B) the electrolyte
C) nephron
D) all of the above

Conductivity and concentration—why are important? Magnesium, sodium, and potassium are very important electrolytes we have in our body when they are at the right level. However, for some patients, these electrolytes may be out of range. Bicarbonate solution is very important and when it is prepared and mix with RO water, we then have dialysate. Conductivity of these electrolytes is measured by the concentration of the solutions. The higher the concentration in the solution, therefore, the more it provides good electrolyte.

The measurement of conductivity of a solution is done by using a conductivity meter, and we have many type of conductivity meters. The most common one is a probe we place in the solution, and we wait until the reading shows up on the display. The second is a phoenix meter. We check for the conductivity in the dialysis machine where we check for pH and conductivity. The main reason for doing that is to verify the total electrical charge of a solution. The dialysis machine has an internal conductivity sensor that displays the actual conductivity in the dialysis machine. The most logical question on the state test would be:

» **The purpose of measuring dialysate conductivity is?**

A) for measuring water RO water conductivity
B) for measuring the internal sensor in the dialysis machine
C) for measuring total electrical charge of a solution
D) all of the above

» **The main components of a nephron are?**

A) veins and arteries that carries blood to the kidneys
B) glomerulus and tubule
C) the kidney, nephron components, and capillaries
D) all of the above

» **The dialysate pH should be:**

A) 4
B) 6
C) 7 to 7.3
D) 12 to 15

Water and the chemicals in it: first let us understand the origin of water. As technicians, we use water, and dialysate needs water to properly mix it. One thing you should understand about water is that at the point it commences to fall, it picks up all sort of contaminants—for instance: germs, bacteria, endotoxins, micro organisms, aluminum, copper, fluoride, calcium, chlorine and chloramine, and pesticides. Other concerns for our drinking water include terrorists who may have tried to contaminate our drinking water. For this reason our water must be clean and treated in an RO, where these contaminant are filtered before we commence to utilize for drinking, cooking, or use for dialysate.

In order to obtain RO water for the purpose of dialysis, the AAMI recommends that we use RO water to filter and remove all dirt and contaminants—that way we can obtain quality water. Why is obtaining RO water so vital? First, as a new technician you must understand that we utilize about 120 to 300 liters of water for only one dialysis treatment and also the amount of hours the patients are in the machine. More time in the machine more water, and also cleaning the machine requires the use of RO water. Hard water syndrome is also a concern; for this reason we utilize a strip in the RO room the to make sure the water we use for dialysate does not contain large amounts of calcium. The purpose of having all these components to great quality water is to ensure that our patients are safe. We also perform another safety procedure, which is that is we check for the total chlorine level in the water before each patient shift, and chemical analysis of water used for hemodialysis is tested annually. All these precautions are taken to make certain the water used for dialysis is safe.

In our RO room some of the components of water treatment are the pre filte which is the sediment filter; the carbon filter, which filters the carbon in the water; water softener, and also reverse osmosis (RO)

Let us have a profound understanding of these filters:

Sediment filters are utilized to remove particles like mud, sand, and rocks from the water.

Carbon filters are utilized to remove chlorine and chloramine.

Water softeners are utilized to remove calcium and magnesium, which are exchanged for sodium salt.

The RO membrane remove the majority of contaminants. It does that by the aid of a membrane and pressure. The most logical question on the state test would be:

» **A lot of calcium in water use for dialysis may cause what ?**

A) uremia in the water syndrome
B) sediment in the water particles syndrome
C) hard water syndrome
D) all of the above

» **Which organization sets the standard and recommendation for dialysis quality water?**

A) Department of State
B) AAMI
C) The Food and Drug Administration
D) all of the above

» **This water is considered to be safe water for dialysis:**

A) carbon water
B) filtered water
C) dialysis-quality water
D) all of the above

» **The water softener removes what from the water?**

A) potassium and sodium
B) calcium and magnesium
C) bicarbonate
D) all of the above

» **Waste products are removed during dialysis by which method ?**

A) concentration gradient
B) ultrafiltration
C) efficient dialyzer
D) osmosis

» **This is diffused from the patient's blood during dialysis:**

A) urea
B) uremia
C) chemicals
D) none of the above

» **The dialysis machine monitors many internal components and alarms us for intervention. Which parameters should be verified by an external component instrument?**

A) blood pressure
B) arterial blood line
C) pH and conductivity
D) all of the above

New dialysis technicians should be aware about kinking blood lines. It is the condition where the venous or arterial blood line is twisted. When this happens, you might have a high venous pressure. For some new technicians, their first temptation is to check the needles and readjust them, when the first thing to do should be look at the blood line to see if there is a twist or kinking. If there is no kinking, stop the blood and properly check your needle insertion, venous or arterial.

» **This may cause a high venous pressure alarm:**

A) high blood flow
B) transmembrane
C) high diffusion
D) kinking of lines

» **The main reason the normal saline is utilized is:**

A) to make sure there is no leak
B) to make sure there is no air.
C) to check for dialysate.
D) All of the above

» **The patient complains of pain at the insertion site. If the technician notice swelling distal to the venous needles site, and in addition, the venous needle is gradually rising, a vigilant technician should assume it is:**

A) recirculation
B) infiltration
C) improper needle placement
D) check the blood pump

» **The following is used in dialysate to maintain a normal pH in the dialysis patient's blood stream?**

A) potassium
B) sodium
C) calcium
D) bicarbonate

» **When do we test for total chlorine levels in water use for dialysis?**

A) every year
B) every month
C) before each patient shift
D) before a patient starts their dialysis

» **According to the AAMI, chemical analysis of water used for hemodialysis should be tested:**

A) weekly
B) monthly
C) twice a year
D) annually

Let have a comprehension as to why aluminum is added to our drinking water ? We know micro organisms are the invisible enemy to our health. Where do you find them? In water, especially drinking water, which includes viruses, bacteria, and protozoa. In some quantities these organism can cause illness, which includes severe diarrhea and fever. These bacteria are difficult to remove from water; however, water treatment with aluminum sulfate is effective at removing these micro organisms.

Water that we drink contains micro organisms that have a negative electrical charge, and these particles repel each other. In order to have these particles clump together, of course we need to neutralize this negative charge. The way this is done is by adding positive ions like aluminum, which causes the negative particles to form clusters of particles called microflocs. The microflocs can be filtered out of the water treatment system with sand filtration. That is why it is important to start the RO system as early as possible—and rinsing our dialysis machine is vital.

» **Which element is more effective in neutralizing certain particles (viruses and bacteria) in comparison to chlorination?**

   A) metal
   B) filtration
   C) aluminum sulfate
   D) coagulation

If you are reading this book as a new technician, you should memorize these alarm terms because you will have to respond to these alarms every now and then. Your quick response is vital to the well-being of the patient. These alarms are vital in order to ensure the safety of the patient.

Air detector alarm: This alarm monitors the blood in the venous line. This line returns blood to the patient's blood stream. If the air detector is activated, it is because it may sense air in the line.

Blood leak detector: This sensor monitors blood leaking out of the dialyzer and into the dialysate solution.

Temperature sensor: This measures the temperature of the dialysate. If the temperature is cold an alarm will sound, so that proper temperature can be adjusted.

Conductivity: This sensor measures the concentration of the mixed chemical in the dialysate solution.

Venous pressure. :The pressure in the blood tubing between the blood pump and venous needles. This pressure should always be positive due to the fact that the pump is pushing the blood back into your needle.

Arterial sensor: There is a pressure in the arterial blood line between the arterial needle and the blood pump. This pressure is negative because the pump is pulling the blood from the needle. If the pump is pulling the faster than the needle can handle, an alarm will be activated. This alarm will cause the blood pump to cease running.

The most logical question on the state test would be:

» **What is the purpose of the air detector on the dialysis machine?**

   A) to detect the presence of air in the urea
   B) to detect the presence of air in the dialysate
   C) to detect the presence of air in the dialysis machine
   D) to detect the presence of air in the blood line

New technicians should be aware and know the parts of the dialysis machine. Here is a list of some of the important parts you should know. You may ask any technician about these parts and their functions.

Here is a list of the parts you should know on the dialysis machine.

   – Touch Screen (that is the computer)
   – Module compartment
   – Concentrate supply lines
   – Acid port
   – IV pole (contains a grip to adjust height)
   – Dialyzer holder
   – Fluid sample port
   – Wheel lock

The reset button on the dialysis machine is utilized to restart the dialysis machine. A new technician should understand that the reset button should be utilized only after you visually observe the patient. This is the time to also communicate and ask your patient, "How are you?" or "Do you feel all right?" As a new technician, when the dialysis machines stop, there is a cause— it could either be the patient moved the access, or something is happening. The best thing you can do is communicate with your patient. Second, read the computer screen on the dialysis machine. If the screen show writing that indicates arterial, it could be that the arterial needle needs adjustment, or if the computer screen indicates venous, it could be the venous chamber needs heparin. You can ask the charge nurse to administer it. It is vital to read the computer screen before attempting to just press the reset button.

The mute button—its purpose is that at some point you may be fixing or adjusting the venous or arterial needle; therefore, you may need to stop the blood pump and clamp the lines so that you can adjust the needles from the patient access. While you are in the process of adjusting the needles, the alarm might sound. At this point you would need to press the mute button. It is very important you do that, so that you can concentrate and allow those patients who are reading a book not to be annoyed by the machine alarm.

» **What is the purpose of the blood leak detector?**

A) the blood leak detector monitor the blood on the access lines
B) monitor the blood inside the dialyzer
C) monitor the blood on the arterial line
D) monitor the venous chamber

» **The conductivity sensor measures what?**

A) measures the urea
B) measures the dialysate solution
C) measures the pH
D) measures the TMP

» **If the venous chamber appears cloudy, you should:**

A) adjust the venous needles
B) call the charge nurse
C) communicate with the patient
D) all of the above

» **The pressure in the arterial blood line between the arterial needle and blood pump is:**

A) weak pressure
B) strong pressure
C) negative pressure
D) all of the above

» **The venous pressure in the blood tubing between the blood pump and venous needle is:**

A) strong pressure
B) weak pressure
C) pulling pressure
D) positive pressure

» **The temperature sensor measures what?**

A) the patient temperature
B) the dialysate temperature
C) the RO temperature
D) all of the above

The air detector alarm monitors:

A) the air in the arterial line
B) the air in the venous line
C) the air in the venous chamber
D) all of the above

The most common dialysis machine you would find on most dialysis units would be a frecinous. If you look at all the details on the surface of the machine, you will see the computer screen which would have the following:

- Arterial pressure
- Venous pressure
- TMT
- Tx running
- UF Goal
- UF Time
- UF Rate
- UF Remove
- Dialysate
- Temperature
- Conductivity
- RTD
- Time: this button is use to enter the patient time in the computor.
- Heparin :
- Blood: Pressure
- Home: Press this button to return to the main screen of the computer.

If you look on the left side on a modern frecinous dialysis machine, you will see a small key pad There you will see the following:

- New Tx : to start the patient treatment.
- UF / OFF This button is to start removal of fluid.
- Prime: This button is used to start priming the blood lines and dialyzer.
- Mute: This button is use to silence the alarm for a while.

Below the key pad you see the following :

- Transducer: A device inside the dialysis machine that change air pressure to an electronic signal. With more advanced blood lines, a transducer is not needed.
- <u>Reset</u>
- Start / Stop: These are used to start Yx treatment or stop treatment.

Section A Date _____

Patient # 100 Pre Weight _____ Post weight _____

Patient # 200 Pre Weight _____ Post Weight _____

Patient # 300 Pre Weight _____ Post Weight _____

Patient # 400 Pre Weight _____ Post Weight _____

New Patient / Visitor

Patient #_____   Pre Weight _____
                               Post Weight _____

Patient # _____   Pre weight _____
                               Post Weight _____

Section B Date _____

Patient # 001 Pre weight _____ Post Weight _____

Patient # 002 Pre Weight _____ Post Weight _____

Patient # 003 Pre Weight _____ Post Weight _____

Patient # 004 Pre Weight _____ Post Weight _____

Patient # 005 Pre Weight _____ Post Wight _____

Visitor/ New Patient

Visitor Patient #_____ Pre Weight _____
                         Post Weight _____

Visitor Patient # _____ Pre Weight _____
                          Post Weight _____

                    # _____ Pre Weight _____
                             Post Weight _____

Section C

Patient # _____   Pre Weight _____
                        Patient Post Weight _____

Patient # _____   Pre Weight _____
                        Patient Post Weight _____

Patient # _____   Pre Weight _____
                        Patient Post Weight _____

Patient# _____   Pre Weight _____
                        Patient Post Weight _____

Patient # _____   Pre Weight _____
                        Patient Post Weight _____

Visitor / New Patient

Patient # _____   Pre Weight _____
                        Patient Post Weight _____

Patient # _____   Pre Weight _____
                        Patient Post Weight _____

      # _____   Pre Weight _____
                        Patient Post Weight _____

Section _____

Patient #_____   Pre Weight _____
                         Patient Post Weight _____

Patient # _____   Pre Weight _____
                         Patient Post Weight _____

Patient # _____   Pre Weight _____
                         Patient Post Weight _____

Patient # _____   Pre Weight _____
                         Patient Post Weight _____

Patient # _____   Pre Weight _____
                         Patient Post Weight _____

Patient # _____   Pre Weight _____
                         Patient Post Weight _____

Patient # _____   Pre weight _____
                         Patient Post Weight _____

Patient # _____   Pre Weight _____
                         Patient Post Weight _____

Patient # _____   Pre Weight _____
                         Patient Post Weight _____

Patient# _____   Pre Weight _____
                        Patient Post Weight _____

Patient # _____   Pre Weight _____
                        Patient Post Weight _____

New info/ up to date information / live 2015

It is important to comprehend your role and what to do when you are helping a patient who is not compliant and your role as a vigilant technician. The parameters of reporting guidelines is vital. As a team, it takes a team approach to care for your patient. I had observed a doctor who is well-experienced with come in doing his round pick up on a patient weight removal, and make adjustment immediately to prevent further problems and complications. He suggested that we should increase the patient removal goal or a bp that might too low, and suggested we should lower the goal. This was a good move on the doctor's part and good practice. As a team we should rely on each other to get the job done well.

As a vigilant technician, you must communicate with your patients. If your co-technician goes on a break, you must do rounds and obtain a verbal communication. Document the verbal response from the patient and take appropriate action.

In the absence of your co-technician, you must do your rounds and document how your patient is doing.

This is a team approach—not just a "my patient only" mentality. So what do you do when your co-technician is on his /her lunch break is that a good technician would fulfill the role of his partner. In order to show you covered your co-technician while on break, you communicate and document how the patient is doing. What does it really indicate if you show any type of documentation while your co-worker is on break? A proactive nurse will also communicate and document for their patients.

What it shows when your co-worker is on a break and your signature and documentation are nowhere to be found on a report log, it simply indicates that you did not communicate with you're the for the whole treatment in any event you encounter some difficulty with an access which you trust might take a some time to resolve communicate with a charge nurse to come to your aid. A proactive nurse would pick up on you emergency right the way and come to your aid, this profession is not I repeat not a competition we are caring for people who need our help. If something happened we all would look bad. This is a(Team) approach profession.

There is no cure for our patients who have kidney failure. Some patients have a few weeks or less than a year to live. Our job is to add few more days to their life, and help our patients while you have the ability, health, and courage to do so.

Note the parameter reporting guidelines.

Understand these parameters:
- If the pre weight is above EDW, but <6kg over last weight this is okay.
- If post treatment weight is 0. 5kg < or >EDW this is okay.
- If Temperature 96-99 degrees F that is okay.
- Heart rate 60 -100 this is okay
- Respirations 16-24 this is okay breaths / minute
- Blood pressure pre treatment <140/90
- w.ufo. tech

ANSWER KEY

Dialysis Essential

Page 3 and 4

This is needed to clean the blood and Technician must understand it:
A. particles and uremia
B. chemical
C. fluid removal
D. vascular access   (D)

This dialysis employee play an important role, in the Unit.
A. lab technician
B. dialysis technician
C. the patient advisor
D. all of the above   (B)

To obtain uremia and particles this is needed and it is made of:
A. plastic tube and artery
B. hallow fiber and vein
C. vein or artery
D. all of the above   (C)

Page 6 and 7

This is where particles and Fluid are remove:
A. dialyzer
B. hallow fiber
C. access
D. strong blood flow   (C)

For a patient to have strong blood flow, this must be done from time to time:
A access
B. proper care
C. needles
D. intervention   (D)

This is known as artificial kidney.
A. kidney organ
B. membrane
C dialyzer
D. dialysate   (C)

A medical process that is use when a person kidney are
    damage:
A. dialyzer
B. dialysis
C. dialysate
D. access flow   (B)

What is the ideal place for a patient to do their dialysis?
A. Hospital
B. clinic
C. at home
D. dialysis center   (D)

Page 8

This type of dialysis can be done at home and can be risky
    and high level of commitment is require:
A. hemodialysis
B. peritoneal dialysis
C. hospital dialysis
D. all of the above   (B)

If million of these are damage it can cause kidney failure:
A. dialysate
B. nerve fiber
C. veins
D. nephron   (D)

The kidney play an important role in controlling what?
A. sugar
B. diabetes
C. food intake
D. electrolytes   (D)

Charge particle such as sodium, calcium magnesium are
   known as:
A. chloride
B. uremia
C. protein
D. electrolytes   (D)

This is known as solvent:
A. glucose
B. electrolyte
C. calcium
D. water   (D)

Page 11

The process by which atom molecules and particle move
   from a region in which they are plentiful is ?
A anastomosis
B. electrolyte movement
C. diffusion
D. osmosis   (C)

When fluid move across a semipermeable membrane, this
   process is known as?
A anastomosis
B. calcium
C electrolytes movement
D. osmosis   (D)

Page 13 (D) clearance
Page 16 (C) surface area and molecular weight
Page 16
The fallowing HIV, Hepatitis B hepatitis C are known as
Blood born pathogen

— ANSWER KEY —

Page 19

These are filter organs, they filter 120 to 150 quarts of blood:
A. dialyzer
B. filtration
C. organs
D. kidneys   (D)

The kidney produce 1 to 2 quarts of waste products and fluid
   then the was product become wat?
A osmosis
B. solute
C. uremia
D. urine   (D)

Page 21

To help the body repair muscles and fight disease the body
   need what?
A calcium
B. potassium
C. Protein
D. sodium   (C)

Dialysis essential

Page 21

Having 20 to 40 percent kidney function is known as?
A. kidney impair
B. nephron
C. chronic kidney disease
D. all of the above   (C)

Page 22

The most likely cause of anemia Is:
A. decrease protein
B. decrease epogen production
C. decrease of normal cell
D. all of the above   (B)

What is the purpose of given ion and epogen to dialysis
   patients ?
A. to raise ion level
B. raise blood electrolytes
C. to raise patient hematocrit level
D. to raise glucose level   (C)

What is the best way to give ion to dialysis patients ?.
A. Pills
B. eating food rich in ion
C. intravenously
D. all of the above   (c)

Page 23

This indicate the amount of ion store in the body:
A. hematocrit score
B. hemoglobin score
C. Ion level
D. the ferritin score   (D)

This score should not be no more than 100 micro grams per
   liter
A hemoglobin score
B. ferritin
C. plasma
D. epogen score   (B)

TSAT score should be score should be between:
A. 70 to 80
B .40 to 50
C. 20 to 50
D all of the above   (C)

A patient who is anemic would have low of what?
A. hemoglobin
B. low electrolytes
C. red blood cells
D. low protein   (C)

Healthy kidney produce this hormone to stimulate bone
   morrow to produce red blood cells.
A erythropoietin
B. (E P O)
C. calcitrol
D. protein   (A)

Page 24

This increase a patient risk to have heart ,kidneys problem
   and to have a stroke:
A anemia
B. low iron
C. high blood pressure
D. low calcium   (C)

If the kidneys are not working properly they release too
   much of what?
A calcitrol
B. sodium
C. uremia
D. renin   (D)

Page 25

What are the cause of diabetes?
A. high fat diet
B. high calcium
C. no insulin production
D. law blood sodium   (C)

Page 26

The hormone insulin insulin controls the level of what?
A. Protein
B. Sugar
C. Hormone
D. Calcium   (B)

When the body does not make insulin this is known as type :
A. low horme
B. low renin
C. type 1 diabetes
D. law calcitrol   (C)

When the body make insulin and cannot utilize it this is
   known as:
A. A low red blood cell
B. low albumin
C. low calcium
D Type 2 diabetes   (D)

Page 27

What is the best way to lower blood sugar ?
A. stay away from sugar
B. limit sugar intake
C. lose weight
D. avoid sugary drink   (c)

Having high blood glucose could cause what?
A. low albumin
B. nerves damage
C. low energy
D. all of the above   (B)

This type of diabetes which cause pain , loss of feeling in toes,
    feet, legs hands and arms.
A. autonomic neuropathy
B. diabetes neuropathy
C. focal neuropathy
D. peripheral   (B)

Page 30

This causes changes in digestion, bladder function ,eyes, lungs
    and causes hypoglycemia.
A. focal neuropathy
B. peripheral neuropathy
C. autonomic neuropathy
D. all of the above   (C)

This cause muscle weakness or pain in any part of the body:
A. peripheral neuropathy
B. focal neuropathy
C. hypoglycemia
D. autonomic   (B)

If the patient has shakiness sweating and palpitations this
    could be the cause of :
A. autonomic neuropathy
B. hypoglycemia
C. low calcium
D. peripheral   (B)

The most common cause of diabetes is ?
A. autonomic neuropathy
B. focal neuropathy
C. peripheral
D. insulin   (C)

Page 32

Patient who stop smoking will reduce the risk of which type of
   diabetes :
A. focal diabetes
B. autonomic
C. type 2 diabetes
D. type 1 diabetes   (C)

Page 41
The body Temperature taken orally should be?   (d)

Page 43   (C)
Page 45   (D)
Page 47   (B)
Page 52   (D)
Page 53   (D)
Page 57   (D)
Page 58   (B)
Page 59   (B)
Page 59   (B)
Page 60   (A)
Page 63   (D)

Page 64   (C)
Page 65   (B)
Page 67   (D)
Page 68   (C)
Page 69   (A)
Page 71   (B)
Page 73   (B)
Page 74   (D)

Page 75   (C)
Page 77   (D)
Page 79   (D)
Page 79   (A)
Page 81   (D)
Page 81   (A)
Page 84   (A)
Page 86   (A)

Page 87

HTC normal range 30 to 33
Hgb normal ranfge 11 to 12
SAT normal range 20 to 50

Page 87
The device used to have an actual dry weight. (C) crit line

Page 88 Ph 6.8 to 7.6

Page 88/ 89
35 degree to 42
Conductivity 13.4 to 14.3

Page 90 (C)

Page 91
Factor that affect clearance   (C)
Recommended range for(Ph)   (B)
Dialysate temperature   (A)

Page 92 (A) 13.4 to 14.3
(A)
(A)
(A)

Page 93
(A) 20 to 50
(C) arterial line section before the blood pump.
Page 94 (C)

Page 95   (C)
Page 95   (C)
Page 95   (A) heparin minimize
Page 96   (D)
Page 97   (D)
Page 97   Semipermeable membrane is a porous wall.
Page 97   Blood and dialysate move in opposite direction
Page 98   (B)
Page 100   (C)
Page 103   (D)
Page 104   (B)
Page 106   (C)
Page 106   (C) normal range for phosphorus level   5.5
Page 107   (D)
Page 108   (C) Diabetes
Page 109   (C)
Page 110   (C) Nephrons
Page 111
(C) Measure total electrical charge
The main components of a nephrons are? (B) Glomerulus
     and tubule
The dialysate ph should be (C) 7 to 7.3\
Page 114   (C) Hard Water
Page 114   (B) Arm I
Page 115   (B) Calcium and Magnesium
Page 115   (A) Waste product are remove during dialysis
                       by which method
Page 115   (B) Uremia
Page 116   (B) Ph MD conductivity
Page 116   KinKing Lines
Page 117   (B) No air
Page 117   (D) normalphin dialysis (bi carbonate)
Page 118   (C) Before coch patient shift
Page 119   (C) Aluminum Sufate
Page 120   To defect air in the blood
Page 123   Monitor blood in the dialysis and dialysate
Page 123   Measure
Page 123   (D) all A the above if the venous appear cloudy
Page 124   (C) Negative pressure
Page 124   the venous pressure positive pressure

Page 124   the temperature sensor meant what

Page 124   the air detector alarm monitors (B) Air I the
venous line

Lightning Source UK Ltd.
Milton Keynes UK
UKOW03f2115060217
293747UK00001B/10/P